Data Lakes

To Christine Collet

Databases and Big Data Set

coordinated by
Dominique Laurent and Anne Laurent

Volume 2

Data Lakes

Edited by

Anne Laurent
Dominique Laurent
Cédrine Madera

WILEY

First published 2020 in Great Britain and the United States by ISTE Ltd and John Wiley & Sons, Inc.

ISTE Ltd
27-37 St George's Road
London SW19 4EU
UK

www.iste.co.uk

John Wiley & Sons, Inc.
111 River Street
Hoboken, NJ 07030
USA

www.wiley.com

Library of Congress Control Number: 2019954836

British Library Cataloguing-in-Publication Data
A CIP record for this book is available from the British Library
ISBN 978-1-78630-585-5

Contents

Preface

This book is part of a series entitled Database and Big Data (DB & BD), the content of which is motivated by the radical and rapid evolution (not to say revolution) of database systems over the last decade. Indeed, since the 1970s – inspired by the relational database model – many research topics have emerged in the database community, such as: deductive databases, object-oriented databases, semi-structured databases, resource description framework (RDF), open data, linked data, data warehouses, data mining and, more recently, cloud computing, NoSQL and Big Data, to name just a few. Currently, the last three issues are increasingly important and attract most research efforts in the domain of databases. Consequently, considering Big Data environments must now be handled in most current applications, the goal of this series is to address some of the latest issues in such environments. By doing so, in addition to reporting on specific recent research results, we aim to provide the readers with evidence that database technology is changing significantly, so as to face important challenges imposed in most applications. More precisely, although relational databases are still commonly used in traditional applications, it is clear that most current Big Data applications cannot be handled by relational database management systems (RDBMSs), mainly because of the following reasons:

– efficiency when facing Big Data in a distributed and replicated environment is now a key issue that RDBMSs fail to achieve, in particular when it comes to joining big-sized tables;

– there is a strong need for considering heterogeneous data, structured, semi-structured or even unstructured, for which no common schema exists.

– Data warehouses are not flexible enough to handle such a variety of data and usages.

Data lakes appeared a couple of years ago in industrial applications and are now deployed in most of the big companies for valorizing the data.

More recently, academic scientists focused their interest on this concept and proposed several contributions to formalizing and exploiting data lakes, but the scientific literature is not yet very rich.

In this book, we try to bring together several points of view on this emerging concept by proposing a panorama.

This book is a tribute to our departed friend and colleague Christine Collet.

Anne LAURENT
Dominique LAURENT
Cédrine MADERA
December 2019

Introduction to Data Lakes: Definitions and Discussions

As stated by Power [POW 08, POW 14], a new component of information systems is emerging when considering *data-driven decision support systems*. This is the case because enhancing the value of data requires that information systems contain a new *data-driven* component, instead of an information-driven component[1]. This new component is precisely what is called *data lake*.

In this chapter, we first briefly review existing work on data lakes and then introduce a global architecture for information systems in which data lakes appear as a new additional component, when compared to existing systems.

1.1. Introduction to data lakes

The interest in the emerging concept of data lake is increasing, as shown in Figure 1.1, which depicts the number of times the expression "data lake" has been searched for during the last five years on Google. One of the earliest research works on the topic of data lakes was published in 2015 by Fang [FAN 15].

Chapter written by Anne LAURENT, Dominique LAURENT and Cédrine MADERA.

1 https://www.gartner.com/smarterwithgartner/the-key-to-establishing-a-data-driven-culture/.

The term *data lake* was first introduced in 2010 by James Dixon, a Penthao CTO, in a blog [DIX 10]. In this seminal work, Dixon expected that data lakes would be huge sets of row data, structured or not, which users could access for sampling, mining or analytical purposes.

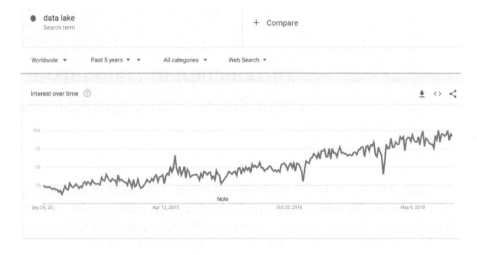

Figure 1.1. *Queries about "data lake" on Google*

In 2014, Gartner [GAR 14] considered that the concept of data lake was nothing but a new way of storing data at low cost. However, a few years later, this claim was changed[2], based on the fact that data lakes have been considered valuable in many companies [MAR 16a]. Consequently, Gartner now considers that the concept of data lake is like a *graal* in information management, when it comes to innovating through the value of data.

In the following, we review the industrial and academic literature about data lakes, aiming to better understand the emergence of this concept. Note that this review should not be considered as an exhaustive, state of the art of the topic, due to the recent increase in published papers about data lakes.

2 https://www.gartner.com/webinar/3745620.

1.2. Literature review and discussion

In [FAN 15], which is considered one of the earliest academic papers about data lakes, the author lists the following characteristics:

– storing data, in their native form, at low cost. Low cost is achieved because (1) data servers are cheap (typically based on the standard X86 technology) and (2) no data transformation, cleaning and preparation is required (thus avoiding very costly steps);

– storing various types of data, such as blobs, data from relational DBMSs, semi-structured data or multimedia data;

– transforming the data only on exploitation. This makes it possible to reduce the cost of data modeling and integrating, as done in standard data warehouse design. This feature is known as the *schema-on-read* approach;

– requiring specific analysis tools to use the data. This is required because data lakes store row data;

– allowing for identifying or eliminating data;

– providing users with information on data provenance, such as the data source, the history of changes or data versioning.

According to Fang [FAN 15], no particular architecture characterizes data lakes and creating a data lake is closely related to the settlement of an Apache Hadoop environment. Moreover, in this same work, the author anticipates the decline of decision-making systems, in favor of data lakes stored in a cloud environment.

As emphasized in [MAD 17], considering data lakes as outlined in [FAN 15] leads to the following four limitations:

1) only Apache Hadoop technology is considered;

2) criteria for preventing the movement of the data are not taken into account;

3) data governance is decoupled from data lakes;

4) data lakes are seen as data warehouse "killers".

In 2016, Bill Inmon published a book on a data lake architecture [INM 16] in which the issue of storing useless or impossible to use data is addressed. More precisely, in this book, Bill Inmon advocates that the data lake architecture should evolve towards information systems, so as to avoid storing only row data, but also "prepared" data, through a process such as ETL (Extract-Transform-Load) that is widely used in data warehouses. We also stress that, in this book, the use of metadata and the specific profile of data lake users (namely that of data scientists) are emphasized. It is proposed the data is organized according to three types, namely *analog data, application data* and *textual data*. However, the issue of how to store the data is not addressed.

In [RUS 17], Russom first mentioned the limitations of Apache Hadoop technology as being the only possible environment of data lakes, which explains why Russom's proposal is based on a hybrid technology, i.e. not only on Apache Hadoop technology but also on relational database technology. Therefore, similar to data warehouses, a few years after Fang's proposal [FAN 15], data lakes are now becoming multi-platform and hybrid software components.

The work in [SUR 16] considers the problems of data lineage and traceability before their transformation in the data lake. The authors propose a baseline architecture that can take these features into account in the context of huge volumes of data, and they assess their proposal through a prototype, based on Apache Hadoop tools, such as Hadoop HDFS, Spark and Storm. This architecture is shown in Figure 1.3, from which it can be seen that elements of the IBM architecture (as introduced in [IBM 14] and shown in Figure 1.2) are present.

In [ALR 15], the authors introduced what they call *personal data lake*, as a means to query and analyze personal data. To this end, the considered option is to store the data in a single place so as to optimize data management and security. This work thus addresses the problem of data confidentiality, a crucial issue with regard to the *General Data Protection Regulation*[3].

---

3 According to Wikipedia, the General Data Protection Regulation (GDPR) "is a regulation in the EU on data protection and privacy for all individuals within the European Union and the European Economic Area."

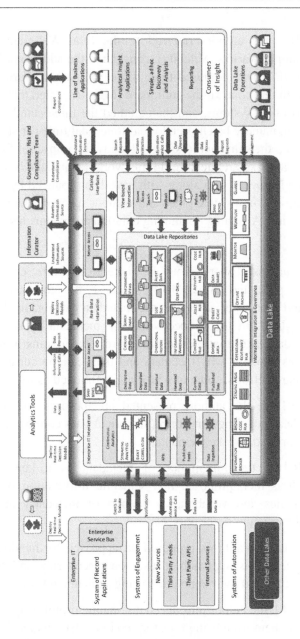

Figure 1.2. *Baseline architecture of a data lake as proposed by IBM [IBM 14]. For a color version of this figure, see www.iste.co.uk/laurent/data.zip*

In [MIL 16], the authors referred to the three Vs cited by Gartner [GAR 11] (Volume, Variety, Velocity), considered the additional V (Veracity) introduced by IBM and proposed three more Vs, namely Variability, Value and Visibility. In this context, the authors of [MIL 16] stated that the data lake should be part of IT systems, and then studied the three standard modes for data acquisition, namely batch pseudo real time, real time (or streaming) and hybrid. However, the same authors did not study the impact of these different modes on the data lake architecture. In this work, a data lake is seen as a data pool, gathering historical data along with new data produced by some pseudo real-time processes, in a single place and without specific schema, as long as data is not queried. A catalog containing data lineage is thus necessary in this context.

The most successful work about data lake architecture, components and positioning is presented in [IBM 14], because the emphasis is on data governance and more specifically on the metadata catalog. In [IBM 14], the authors highlighted, in this respect, that the metadata catalog is a major component of data lakes that prevents them from being transformed into data "swamps". This explains why metadata and their catalog currently motivate important research efforts, some of which are mentioned as follows:

– in [NOG 18a], the authors presented an approach to data vault (an approach to data modeling for storing historical data coming from different sources) for storing data lake metadata;

– in [TER 15], the importance of metadata as a key challenge is emphasized. It is then proposed that semantic information obtained from domain ontologies and vocabularies be part of metadata, in addition to traditional data structure descriptions;

– in [HAI 16], the authors proposed an approach for handling metadata called *Constance*. This approach focuses on discovering and summarizing structural metadata and their annotation using semantic information;

– in [ANS 18], the author introduced a semantic profiling approach to data lakes to prevent them from being transformed into "data swamps". To this end, it is shown that the semantic web provides improvements to data usability and the detection of integrated data in a data lake.

Regarding data storage, in [IBM 14], it is argued that the exclusive use of Apache Hadoop is now migrating to hybrid approaches for data storage (in particular using relational or NoSQL techniques, in addition to Apache Hadoop), and also for platforms (considering different servers either locally present or in the cloud). As mentioned earlier, these changes were first noted in [RUS 17].

An attempt to unify these different approaches to data lakes can be found in [MAD 17] as the following definition:

A *data lake* is a collection of data such that:

– the data have no fixed schema;

– all data formats should be possible;

– the data have not been transformed;

– the data are conceptually present in one single place, but can be physically distributed;

– the data are used by one or multiple experts in data science;

– the data must be associated with a metadata catalog;

– the data must be associated with rules and methods for their governance.

Based on this definition, the main objective of a data lake is to allow for a full exploitation of its content for providing value to the data in the company. In this context, the data lake is a data-driven system that is part of the decision-making system.

1.3. The data lake challenges

Initially regarded as low-cost storage environments [GAR 14], data lakes are now considered by companies as strategic tools due to their potential ability to give data a high value [MAR 16b].

As shown in Figure 1.4, data lake selling is rapidly increasing. It is expected that sales would reach the amount of $8.81 billion in 2021, with an increase of 32.1%.

Reference Architecture

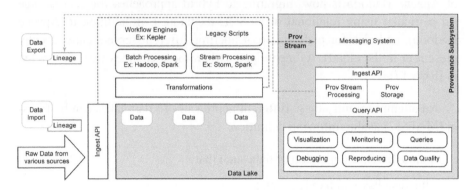

Figure 1.3. *Baseline architecture of a data lake of [SUR 16]*

Data Lakes Market	2014	2015	2016-e	2021-p	CAGR (2016–2021)
Market Size	1.82	2.12	2.53	8.81	28.3%
Y-o-Y		16.3%	19.5%	32.1%	

e – Estimated; p – Projected

Note: Y-o-Y for the year 2021 has been calculated from 2020-2021

Source: Press Releases, Investor Presentations, Expert Interviews, and MarketsandMarkets Analysis

Figure 1.4. *Data lake software prices*

In the report [MAR 16b], on the analysis of worldwide data lake sales, it is argued that the most important problem for increasing these sales is due to a lack of information about novel techniques for storing and analyzing data and about long-term data governance. This report also identifies, in this respect, the problems of data security and data confidentiality, as well as a lack of experts who are able to understand the new challenges related to the increasing importance of data lakes.

On the contrary, the increasing need to fully benefit from their data explains why more and more data lakes are used in companies. In light of the report [MAR 16b], data lakes can be seen as an important and challenging issue for companies, regardless of their size. Figure 1.5 shows an overview of these phenomena.

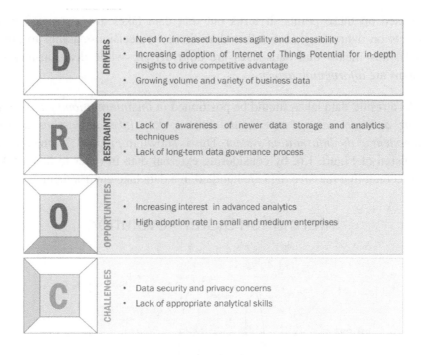

Sources: Secondary Literature, Press Releases, Expert Interviews, and MarketsandMarkets Analysis

Figure 1.5. *Data lake sales: positive and negative aspects and challenges. For a color version of this figure, see www.iste.co.uk/laurent/data.zip*

We now study how to position data lakes in information systems, based on Le Moigne's approach [LEM 84].

Summarizing the works in [FAN 15, IBM 14, HAI 16, RUS 17, NOG 18a], the following points should be considered:

– the importance of metadata management;

– the importance of handling data security and confidentiality;

– the importance of handling the data lifecycle;

– the importance of data lineage and data processing.

Based on these points, it turns out that data lakes are associated with projects on data governance rather than those on decision-making. In other words, this means that data lakes are *data driven*, while decision-making systems are *information driven*.

As a result, data lakes should be positioned *in the information system, next to the decision-making system*, and thus *a data lake appears as a new component of the information system*. This is shown in Figure 1.7, which is an expansion of Figure 1.6, by considering external data in order to better take into account that massive data are handled in a data lake environment.

Information System evolution

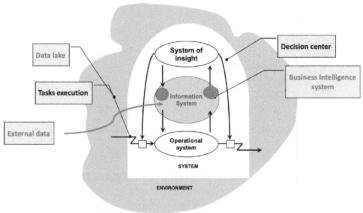

Figure 1.6. *Data lake position in the information system. For a color version of this figure, see www.iste.co.uk/laurent/data.zip*

1.4. Data lakes versus decision-making systems

While we previously discussed the positioning of the data lake inside the information system, we now emphasize the differences between data lakes and decision-making systems.

Data lakes are often compared to data warehouses because both concepts allow for storing huge volumes of data in order to transform them into information. However, data lakes are expected to be more flexible than data warehouses, because data lakes do *not* impose that data are integrated according to the same schema. Therefore, any data can be inserted in a data lake, regardless of their nature and origin, which implies that one of the major challenges is to allow for any processing dealing with these data[4].

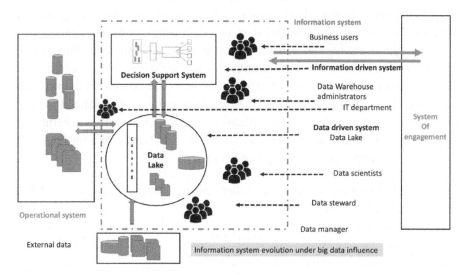

Figure 1.7. *Data lake interaction in information systems. For a color version of this figure, see www.iste.co.uk/laurent/data.zip*

This way of integrating data differs from data integration in data warehouses in the sense that data lakes are said to be *schema on read*, whereas data warehouses are said to be *schema on write*. This terminology illustrates that:

– in a data warehouse, the schema is fixed before integration because the expected information is known in advance. This explains why, in the case of a data warehouse, the different steps of data integration are known as ETL (Extract-Transform-Load);

– in a data lake, the information to be extracted from the integrated data is totally unknown, and it is up to the user to express his or her needs, and thus it

4 https://www.cigref.fr/publications-numeriques/ebook-cigref-entreprise-2020-enjeux-defis/index.html.

is up to the user to define the needed data schema. This explains why the data integration steps for a data lake are known as ELT (Extract-Load-Transform).

It is important to note that to ensure data veracity when integrating several sources, data cleaning is a crucial step. In a data warehouse environment, this step is achieved during the transformation process, i.e. before loading, which is not possible in a data lake environment, since the data are transformed "on demand" after loading. However, in practice, in a data lake environment, data cleaning may also be achieved on loading through normalization and extraction of the metadata. This explains the importance of data governance, and more specifically of the maintenance of a metadata catalog, when it comes to guaranteeing data lineage and veracity.

In conclusion, the main differences between data warehouses and data lakes are summarized in Table 1.1.

	Data lakes	Data warehouses
Data storage	HDFS, NoSQL, Relational database	Relational database
Data qualification	No	Yes
Data value	High	High
Data granularity	Raw	Aggregated
Data preparation	On the fly	Before integration
Data integration	No treatment	Quality control, filtering
Data transformation	No transformation ELT	Transformation ETL
Schema	On read	On write
Information architecture	Horizontal	Vertical
Model	On the fly	Star, snowflake
Metadata	Yes	Optional
Conception	Data driven	Information driven
Data analysis method	Unique	Repetitive
Users	Computer/data scientists, developers	Decision-makers
Update frequency	Real time/batch	Batch
Architecture	Centralized, federated or hybrid	Centralized

Table 1.1. *Data warehouses versus data lakes*

1.5. Urbanization for data lakes

According to Servigne [SER 10], *urbanization* of an information system should provide users and information providers with a common view of the information system, and moreover, urbanization should ensure that the information system supports the goals and the transformation of the company, while reducing expenses and easing the implementation of evolution and strategy changing.

The expected outcomes of urbanization for the information system are more precisely stated as follows:

– make the system responsive to the global business project;

– align the information system with strategic targets;

– ensure consistency between data and processes;

– easily take into account technological innovations;

– provide full value to the data and the knowledge in the information system;

– reduce the costs of maintenance and exploitation;

– improve the functional quality;

– improve the quality of service;

– make data more reliable;

– make the information system flexible.

Referring to "urbanization", as used in architecture and geography, the goal of "urbanizing" the information system is to structure the system so as to improve its performance and upgradability. As shown in Figure 1.8, the process of "urbanizing" the information system is achieved using the following four-layer model:

1) the business architecture;

2) the functional architecture;

3) the application architecture;

4) the technical architecture.

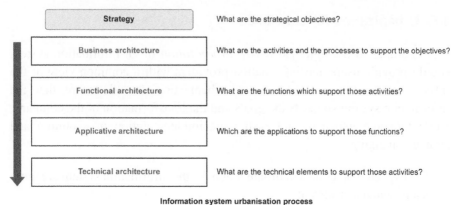

Figure 1.8. *Urbanization of the information system*

In the following, we detail these four architectures in the specific case of data lake urbanization.

The *business architecture* of a data lake is about the issue of knowledge capitalization and value, in the goal of digital transformation. Regarding the *functional architecture*, the data lake is meant to collect all data on a single place (with regard to capitalization), at a conceptual level, so as to allow various software tools to exploit them (thus ensuring data value). The functional schema of a data lake can be considered, as shown in Figure 1.9, to guarantee the following needs:

– accessibility to all data sources;

– centralization of all data sources;

– provision of a catalog of available data.

The *applicative architecture* is a computational view of the functional architecture described above. An example of an applicative architecture is shown in Figure 1.10[5], and the main components of such an architecture are listed as follows:

5 Why use a data lake? Retrieved from http://www.jamesserra.com/archive/2015/12/why-use-a-data-lake/.

– data storage: relational DBMSs, NoSQL systems and file systems such as HDFS;

– data manipulation: architecture frameworks such as MapReduce or Apache Spark;

– metadata management: software such as Informatica or IBM Metadata Catalogue;

– suites for data lakes, based on HDFS such as Cloudera or Hortonworks;

– machine learning software such as Apache Spark and IBM Machine Learning.

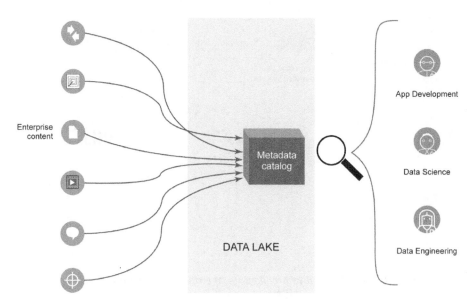

Figure 1.9. *Functional architecture of a data lake*

The *technological architecture* provides the description of the hardware components that support those from the applicative architecture. These components are typically:

– servers;

– workstations;

– storage devices (storage units, SAN, filers, etc.);

– backup systems;

– networking equipment (routers, firewalls, switches, load balancers, SSL accelerators).

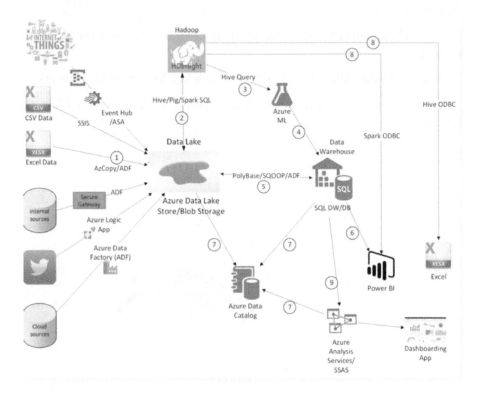

Figure 1.10. *Applicative architecture of a data lake (Hortonworks^{TM}).*
For a color version of this figure, see www.iste.co.uk/laurent/data.zip

The choice of these components is driven by specific needs for data lakes regarding the characteristics of the data to be handled. These needs are mainly:

– security;

– availability;

– scalability;

– auditability;

– performance;

– volume;

– integrity;

– robustness;

– maintenance;

– reliability.

We note in this respect that so far the influence of these needs on the performance of the data lake has not been investigated. This is due to the lack of maturity of most current data lake projects, and it is expected that the importance of the impact of these needs on the technological architecture of data lakes will increase in the near future. As an example of such impact, in this book we address the issue of *data gravity*, by investigating how technological constraints on data storage may impact components of the applicative architecture.

1.6. Data lake functionalities

From our point of view, data lake functionalities should address the following issues: data acquisition, metadata catalog, data storage, data exploration, data governance, data lifecycle and data quality. In this section, we briefly review each of these issues.

The functionality of *data acquisition* deals with data integration from various data sources (internal or external, structured or not). This is much like the ODS (Operation Data Store) component of an industrial decision-making system. As mentioned earlier, this functionality must allow for the integration of any data stream, but another possibility is to merge it with that of the associated decision-making system. This option is shown in Figure 1.11.

Regarding *metadata catalog*, all approaches in [FAN 15, HAI 16, ANS 18, STE 14, IBM 14] put the emphasis on this functionality, because without it, the data lake would be like a data "swamp". As mentioned earlier, metadata are among the most important information in a data lake because they allow for data governance, data security, data quality and lifecycle. Although no consensus exists regarding their format, it is agreed that metadata should provide answers to the following typical questions regarding any piece of data:

– Who created it? Who uses it? Whom does it belong to? Who maintains it?

– What is its business definition? What are its associated business rules? Which is its security level?   Which standard terms define it within the databases?

– Where is it stored? Where is it from? Where is it used or shared? Which regulatory or legal standard does it comply with?

– Why is it stored? What is its usage and utility? What is its associated business lever?

– When has it been created or updated? When will it be erased?

– How has it been formatted?

– In how many databases or data sources can it be found?

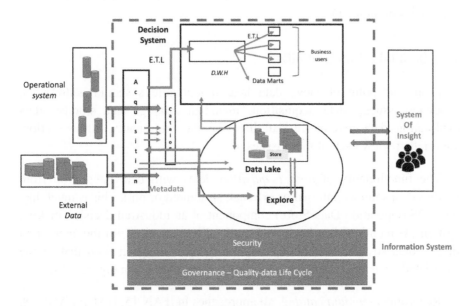

Figure 1.11. *Acquisition module shared between data lake and decision-support system. For a color version of this figure, see www.iste.co.uk/laurent/data.zip*

Among the basic expectations regarding metadata, we mention the following:

– *access to information* by any user, including non-expert users, to collect information on data structure, content or quality;

– *data quality* must be eased so that the user can concentrate on data exploitation rather than on data information;

– *saving time* by providing a full data profile;

– *data security* must be guaranteed, specifically in the context of RGPD regulation regarding personal data;

– *data exploitation* must be eased, in particular through *data lineage* information contained in metadata.

– companies have reservoirs of valuable *hidden data*, which are not exploited. These data can be produced by operating systems or complex applications. Once registered in the data lake with their metadata, these hidden data can be used and maintained properly.

Now turning to *data storage* functionality, we recall that according to [GAR 14] and [FAN 15], a data lake is reduced to data storage using an Apache Hadoop technology; in [RUS 17], the expression "Hadoop Data Lake" is used to refer to these approaches.

As noted previously on Russom's work [RUS 17], alternative and complementary technologies can be used, such as relational or NoSQL DBMSs. When dealing with gravity, we also show that technological and applicative technologies can have a significant impact on this functionality.

The aim of the *data exploration* functionality is to allow users to exploit the content of the data lake. This functionality is significantly different when comparing data lakes and data warehouses. This is because data lake users are fewer and smarter than data warehouse users because data lake technology involves more sophisticated tools and more heterogeneous data than data warehouses.

The *data lake governance* functionality relies on the management of the metadata catalog. However, we stress that security, lifecycle and quality of the data are also fundamental regarding data lake governance. The *data security* functionality deals with data protection, confidentiality and privacy. These are hot topics in the context of data lakes; they are taken into account by rules, processes or ad hoc technologies for data encryption or anonymization.

The *data lifecycle* functionality should make it possible to efficiently manage the data during their "life" in the data lake, starting when they are first stored, used and then ending when they become obsolete and thus are either archived or erased. Such a management is, of course, crucial in a data lake, given the huge volume of data to be managed. To be effective and efficient, this functionality relies on metadata that contain the required information.

The last functionality to be mentioned here is the *data quality* functionality, which is considered challenging in a data lake environment. This is because any type of data can be accepted in a data lake, namely either primary data (which might have been transformed and/or cleaned) or row data (neither transformed nor cleaned). Here again, metadata play a key role in informing the user about the lineage of these data.

1.7. Summary and concluding remarks

As stated previously, [SER 10], the data lake should be considered as a new component of the information system, with its own business, functional, soft and technological architectures, just like any other component. Its content is composed of row data (in their original format) that can be accessed by "smart" users based on specific and innovative tools. A data lake must be agile and flexible, contrary to data warehouses.

In order to avoid the transformation of a data lake into a data "swamp", rules for data governance must be considered in terms of the management of data quality, data security, data lifecycle and of metadata. We emphasize again that the metadata catalog is the key component of the data lake architecture for ensuring the consistency of data sources as well as efficient data governance.

2

Architecture of Data Lakes

In this chapter, we define the most important features of data lake systems, and from there we outline an architecture for these systems. Our vision for a data lake system is based on a generic and extensible architecture with a unified data model, facilitating the ingestion, storage and metadata management over heterogeneous data sources.

We also introduce a real-life data lake system called *Constance* that can deal with sophisticated metadata management over raw data extracted from heterogeneous data sources. Constance discovers, extracts, and summarizes the structural metadata from the data sources, and annotates data and metadata with semantic information to avoid ambiguities. With embedded query rewriting engines that support structured data and semi-structured data, Constance provides users with a unified interface for query processing and data exploration.

2.1. Introduction

Big Data has undoubtedly become one of the most important challenges in database research. An unprecedented volume, a large variety and high velocity of data need to be captured, stored and processed to provide us knowledge. In the Big Data era, the trend of *Data Democratization* brings in a wider range

---

Chapter written by Houssem CHIHOUB, Cédrine MADERA, Christoph QUIX and Rihan HAI.

of users, and at the same time a higher diversity of data and more complex requirements for integrating, accessing and analyzing these data.

However, compared to other Big Data features such as "Volume" and "Velocity" (sometimes also including "Veracity" and "Value"), "Variety" remains a daunting challenge with more widespread issues [ABA 14]. Variety (or heterogeneity) exists at several levels:

– at the instance level: the same entity might be described with different attributes;

– at the schema level: the data might be structured with various schemas [DON 15];

– at the level of the modeling language: different data models can be used (e.g. relational, XML, or a document-oriented JSON representation).

For example, web-based business transactions, sensor networks, real-time streaming, social media and scientific research generate large amounts of semi-structured data and unstructured data, which are often stored in separated information silos. The combination and integrated analysis of the information in these silos often bring the required valuable insight, which is not achievable with an isolated view on a single data source.

However, the heterogeneity of the data sources requires new integration approaches which can handle the large volume and speed of the generated data, as well as the variety of these data. Traditional *"Schema-comes-first"* approaches as in the relational world with data warehouse systems and ETL (Extract-Transform-Load) processes are not appropriate for a flexible and dynamically changing data management landscape.

The requirement for pre-defined, explicit schemas is a limitation which has drawn the interest of many developers and researchers to NoSQL data management systems, because these systems should provide data management features for a high amount of schema-less data. However, even though open-source platforms, such as Hadoop with higher level languages (e.g. Pig and Hive), as well as NoSQL systems (e.g. Cassandra and

MongoDB), are gaining more popularity, the current market share is still dominated by relational systems[1].

Nevertheless, a one-size-fits-all Big Data system is unlikely to solve all the challenges that are required from data management systems today. Instead, multiple classes of systems, optimized for specific requirements or hardware platforms, will co-exist in a data management landscape [ABA 14].

Thus, these new systems do not solve the heterogeneity problem, as they just add new choices for data management, thereby increasing the complexity of a data management landscape, by introducing new data models, new query languages, new APIs and new transaction models. Therefore, the need for an integrated access to all data in organizations is more prominent than before.

As an answer to this, the term *Data Lake* (DL) has been coined recently by IT consulting companies [STE 14][2] and database vendors [CHE 14][3], [TER 15][4]. Various solutions and systems are proposed to address the challenges of a data lake. However, as "data lake" is a current buzzword, there is much hype about it, even though many do not really know what it is. An abstracted definition from the IBM Redbook [CHE 14] is:

> *A data lake is a set of centralized repositories containing vast amounts of raw data (either structured or unstructured), described by metadata, organized into identifiable datasets, and available on demand.*

An important keyword in the context of data lakes is "on-demand", meaning that issues like schema definition, integration, or indexing should be done only if necessary at the time of data access. This might not only increase the cost or effort for accessing the data, but also increase the flexibility for dynamically changing data sources, as it is not necessary to define their schemas and mappings beforehand.

---

1 http://db-engines.com/en/ranking.

2 http://www.gartner.com/it-glossary/data-lake.

3 http://azure.microsoft.com/en-us/campaigns/data-lake/.

4 https://blogs.oracle.com/dataintegration/entry/announcing_oracle_data_integrator_for.

Another important keyword for data lakes is "metadata". As schema information, mappings and other constraints are not defined explicitly and are not required initially. It is important to extract as much metadata as possible from the data sources and if the metadata cannot be extracted from the sources automatically, a human has to provide additional information about the data source. Without any metadata, the data lake is hardly usable because the structure and semantics of the data are not known.

Upon examination of the publications of IT vendors that promote the idea of data lakes, one could fall under the impression that the users of data lakes are wizards who can pull some water from the lake into a cauldron, throw in some magic spices, stir it a little bit and them pull out the magic white rabbit (which is a metaphor for completely integrated datasets or great analytical results). In reality, however, the wizard requires a herd of IT consultants to set up the cauldron, the magic spices cost a lot of money, the stirring takes twice as long as expected, and the result is just an overcooked, lame duck, which nobody wants to eat, because users became vegetarians in the meantime!

We must point out that the initial plans and reality can be very distinct, which is caused not only by false promises of IT vendors, but also by underestimating the complexity of data integration problems [STO 14]. And so, the goal of this chapter is to provide an overview of the current discussion about data lakes from the perspective of database research, especially to point out the new challenges for data management systems. Luckily, we do not have to start from scratch, as many approaches in the area of data integration, semi-structured data and distributed databases apply to data lakes as well. Therefore, here we analyze how existing approaches address the data lake challenges and where additional research is required.

The rest of the chapter is organized as follows: the current state of practice is summarized in section 2.2. Based on this, we describe in section 2.3 an architecture for a data lake system and its most important components. To illustrate such an architecture, we present in section 2.4 the Constance system first introduced in [HAI 16]. Finally, section 2.5 concludes the chapter with a few remarks.

2.2. State of the art and practice

2.2.1. Definition

The first online articles on data lakes in 2010 by James Dixon[5] and in 2011 by Dan Woods [WOO 11] did not immediately receive much attention. Only since some articles[6] took the idea up again in 2013 and early 2014, has the interest in data lakes been growing.

In his initial article (and in his more detailed article from 2014[7]), James Dixon described data lakes as systems that store data from a *single* source in its original, raw format. However, most people consider a data lake today as a system which gets its data from multiple sources.

It is therefore important to introduce some governance about the ingestion process for a data lake. Indeed, a data lake *should be able* to take data from any kind of data source, but in order to avoid being transformed into a data swamp, the data lake has to ingest these data by fulfilling some minimum requirements (e.g. providing metadata and a description of the raw data format). Gartner pointed this out in a criticism of the data lake concept[8]. We note that a proper metadata management is frequently mentioned as a basic requirement for a data lake system, but details about the required metadata services (e.g. model or functions) are often missing.

2.2.2. Architecture

Some architecture models have been proposed. Some are very abstract sketches from industry (e.g. by *pwc* in [STE 14] or by *podium data*[9]), and some are more concrete from research prototypes (e.g. [BOC 15, TER 15, HAA 14]). These proposals usually describe abstracted business data lake systems with conceptual architectures, functional requirements and possible product components. The aforementioned existing

---

5 https://jamesdixon.wordpress.com/2010/10/14/pentaho-hadoop-and-data-lakes/.

6 https://www.ibm.com/developerworks/community/blogs/haraldsmith/entry/big_data_lake_or _big_data_landfill?lang=en.

7 https://jamesdixon.wordpress.com/2014/09/25/data-lakes-revisited/.

8 http://www.gartner.com/newsroom/id/2809117.

9 http://www.podiumdata.com/solutions/.

proposals do not provide the theoretical or experimental support for data lake systems, nor do they provide the details that would enable repeatable implementations. This is the case because these scenario-specific solutions may not apply to a wider usage of data lakes [DOU 15].

As Hadoop is also able to handle any kind of data in its distributed file system, many people think that "Hadoop" is the complete answer to the question of how a data lake should be implemented. Of course, Hadoop is good at managing the huge amount of data in a data lake with its distributed and scalable file system, and Hadoop also provides metadata management functionalities – but, it does not provide all the metadata functionalities required for a data lake. For example, the data lake architecture presented in [BOC 15] shows that a data lake system is a complex eco-system of several components and that Hadoop only provides a part of the required functionality.

2.2.3. *Metadata*

A MetaData Management System (MDMS) for data lakes should provide means to handle metadata in different data models (relational, XML, JSON, RDF), and should be able to represent mappings between the metadata entries. Without the ability to define relationships between the datasets in a data lake, there is the risk that the data lake is just a collection of independent information silos and that it becomes useless over time. Another important requirement for an MDMS in data lakes is the support for *metadata evolution*. Indeed, metadata are added to the data sources over time, and so, semantic annotations about the meaning of some data items could have to be added to the data source metadata [STE 14].

The metadata are also important for querying data lakes. This is because, instead of querying a "relational style" with a predefined schema and precise constraints (as in data warehouses), querying a data lake will also involve an exploration process to detect the data sources which are relevant for a certain information that is needed [WOO 11, STE 14]. Moreover, the annotated metadata should not be only exploited for querying, but should also be further enriched with the information on how data sources are used in queries. Thereby, the metadata are incrementally enriched, thus providing more value to subsequent information needs. This resembles much of the ideas for data space systems [FRA 05], in which heterogeneous data sources are integrated in an incremental and interactive way called "pay-as-you-go integration" [JEF 08]. Data lakes are more general than data spaces as they collect data from an entire organization and not only from one particular user.

Nevertheless, people should not fall into the same trap as many organizations did with their data warehouse projects in the 1990s: it is difficult (if not impossible) to build a meaningful, integrated schema for a large collection of data sources, and this problem will not be solved by the incremental approach of data lakes. The efforts required for data curation (e.g. transformation, integration, cleaning) should not be underestimated [STO 14].

2.2.4. *Data quality*

Another problem mentioned frequently with data lakes is *data quality* [STE 14, STO 14]. As with data warehouses, many data quality problems arise when the data is used in a different context than was originally planned [JAR 99]. Legacy data might be only of limited value outside its usual context, in which specific semantics and workarounds might have been hard-coded into the applications [STE 14]. Therefore, data quality and lineage have to be considered for a data lake system, but standards, reference models and even guidelines are still missing.

2.2.5. *Schema-on-read*

Almost zero-overhead loading is also an assumption (and requirement) stated in the context of data lakes. Loading data in the data lake should not require a significant extra effort. However, in order to avoid the data lake becoming a data swamp, some human efforts are necessary to provide the required metadata for a data source. Furthermore, a data lake system is certainly not able to read all proprietary file formats and extract meaningful schema information and other metadata automatically. Thus, some human effort for the configuration is necessary in this respect. Also, a lazy approach for loading data saves time during the ingestion process, but the configuration work and also the delayed processing of the data have to be done.

Schema-on-read means dynamically creating a schema upon query execution, which may include lazy indexing, view construction or just-in-time query planning [WHI 09, LIU 15, MIT 13]. In contrast to the traditional schema-on-write mechanisms, a data lake system should be able to take any kind of data, even if no schema is available for that data. The reason to apply schema-on-read is that the appropriate way to structure the schema depends on the query/analysis and hence may be unknown at loading time. That the source data is not constrained by schemas defined *a priori* is one of the important features of data lakes, because a predefined schema might limit the later usage scenarios of the data. Schema-on-read techniques may also reduce the indexing effort for data processed just once [RIC 14, ABA 14].

2.3. System architecture

Figure 2.1 depicts a standard proposal for an architecture of a data lake system. As in [SAK 19], the following four layers are considered:

1) the *ingestion layer*;

2) the *storage layer*;

3) the *transformation layer*;

4) the *interaction layer*.

As we do not expect some kind of magic to appear and resolve all the issues (source selection, ingestion, metadata extraction and definition, schema management, etc.) automatically, we envision three main roles of users involved in a data lake system:

1) *data lake administrators* who mainly take care of the ingestion layer by selecting and preparing the sources to be integrated in the data lake;

2) *data scientists* who are the curators of the data lake and prepare the data in such a way that it can be easily queried by the end users;

3) *users* who have requirements which are translated into formal queries with the help of the components at the interaction layer and the data scientists.

In the following sections, we discuss each of the layers and the user roles separately in more detail.

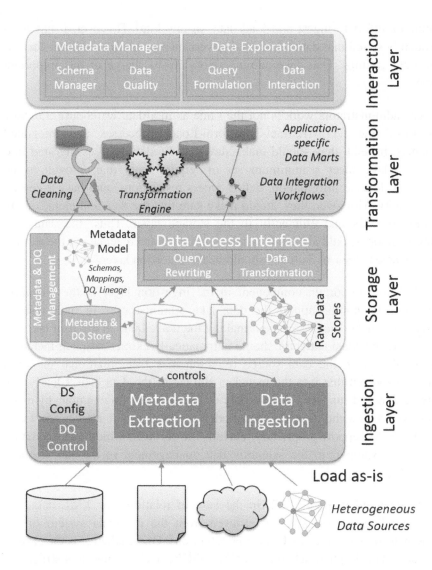

Figure 2.1. *Architecture of a data lake. For a color version of this figure, see www.iste.co.uk/laurent/data.zip*

2.3.1. *Ingestion layer*

This layer is responsible for importing data from heterogeneous sources to the data lake system. One of the key features of the data lake concept is the minimum effort to ingest and load data, of any kind. However, it has been frequently stated that data lakes need governance to avoid being transformed into data swamps. Data lake administrators are in charge of this important issue.

The administrators work is not the same as in a data warehouse, i.e. they do not define ETL (Extract-Transform-Load) processes and integrated schemas. Instead, they should make sure that the data sources ingested into the data lake meet a minimum set of requirements (e.g. provide some metadata, lineage information, define access restrictions) and have a certain data quality. Moreover, they should make sure that the data and metadata are stored correctly and efficiently in the storage layer. Thus, the data lake administrators should also maintain the source-related metadata in the storage layer, whereas their main focus should be the ingestion layer.

The most important component in the ingestion layer is the *metadata extractor*. It should support the data lake administrators in their task of configuring new data sources and making them available in the data lake. To do so, the metadata extractor should automatically extract as much metadata as possible from the data source (e.g. schemas from relational or XML sources) and put that into the metadata storage of the data lake. Clearly, the extractor should support a wide variety of source types, for example, by using frameworks like the Apache Metamodel or Tika, and it also needs to be extensible to support proprietary, custom file formats, which are frequently used, for example, in the scientific data management in the life sciences [BOU 11].

As depicted in Figure 2.2, in the case of relational or XML data, the corresponding schema can be retrieved from the metadata system of the relational source or the XML schema definitions. One challenge is the case of raw data with implicit schemas, such as JSON, text or some less-structured XML. In these cases, the metadata extractor needs to discover entity and relationship types, attributes and constraints (functional dependencies) from semi-structured data [IZQ 13, ARE 14].

In addition to the metadata, the raw data need to be ingested into the data lake. As noted in [SAK 19], since the raw data are kept in their original format, this is more like a "copy" operation, which is certainly less complex than an ETL process in data warehouses. Nevertheless, the data need to be put into the storage layer of the data lake. This might imply some transformation or loading of the data into the "raw data stores" in the storage layer. The loading process can be done in a lazy way, i.e. only if a user requests data from this particular data source [KAR 13].

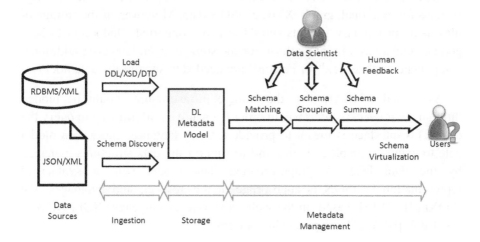

Figure 2.2. *Schema management workflow in a data lake. For a color version of this figure, see www.iste.co.uk/laurent/data.zip*

Finally, the *data quality control* component should make sure that the ingested data have a minimum quality. Note, however, in this respect that due to the huge volume and variety of the data, it might not be possible to specify all data quality rules manually. It is thus necessary to design tools to provide administrators with automatic support to detect such rules and then to evaluate these rules in a fuzzy way [SAH 14].

2.3.2. *Storage layer*

The two main components in the storage layer are the *metadata repository* and the *raw data repositories*.

We refer to Chapter 4 for a detailed discussion about metadata. We simply emphasize here that, as noted in [SAK 19], the *metadata repository* stores all metadata of the data lake which have been partially collected automatically in the ingestion layer or will later be added manually during the curation of the data lake.

However, as noted in [SAK 19], *raw data repositories* being stored in their original format, data lake environments have to provide various storage systems for relational, graph, XML or JSON data. Moreover, as the storage of files using proprietary formats should also be supported, Hadoop is to be a good candidate as a basic platform for the storage layer. However, additional components such as Tez[10] or Falcon[11] are needed to support the data fidelity.

As argued in [SAK 19], the storage infrastructure should be hidden through a *data access interface*, in order to ensure a uniform way to query the data. This interface is meant to provide a query language and a data model able to express complex queries and to support the data structures managed by the data lake. A graph-oriented data model with a syntactical representation in JSON is appropriate in this respect, and languages like JSONiq [FLO 13], based on the well-known query languages SQL, XQuery and JAQL [BEY 11], are promising options.

Although *application-specific data marts* are actually part of the storage layer, it has been pointed out in [SAK 19] that data marts should be considered as part of the interaction layer. This is because data marts are created by the users during their interaction with the data lake. In addition, data marts can be more application-independent if they contain a general-purpose dataset which has been defined by a data scientist. Such a dataset might be useful in many information requests from the users. The storage layer requires a skilled data scientist as a manager, because the complexity of the storage systems and metadata requires advanced data management skills. As in the ingestion layer, the job of the data scientist should be supported by semi-automatic methods (e.g. to support schema creation and integration, definition of indexes, definition of the data marts).

2.3.3. *Transformation layer*

The transformation layer allows data to be prepared from their storage to user interactions: cleansing operations, format transformations, etc.

---

10 http://hortonworks.com/hadoop/tez/.

11 http://falcon.apache.org/.

The users may also wish to create data marts as personal information space, while they are working with the system. Therefore, data marts are logically defined at the interaction layer, prepared at the transformation layer, whereas the data in the data marts will be stored physically in one of the repositories at the storage layer.

2.3.4. *Interaction layer*

Since it cannot be expected that users are able to handle all functionalities offered by the data access system directly, the *interaction layer* should cover all these functionalities that are required to work with the data. As mentioned in [SAK 19], these functionalities should include visualization, annotation, selection and filtering of data, as well as basic analytical methods. It is also important to note, as in [SAK 19], that more complex analytics involving machine learning and data mining should not be considered as part of the functionalities available in a data lake system.

2.4. Use case: the Constance system

To help readers clearly understand the aforementioned architecture and workflow of data lake systems, we give an overview in this section of a data lake prototype called Constance [HAI 16].

2.4.1. *System overview*

Figure 2.3 depicts the architecture of Constance, as well as its key components. Constance can be roughly divided into three functional layers: *ingestion*, *maintenance* and *query*.

While the ingestion layer implements the interface between the data sources and Constance, the major human–machine interaction is enabled by the querying layer. In the middle are the components constituting the maintenance layer, which dynamically and incrementally extract and summarize the current metadata of the data lake, and provide a uniform query interface. These functional layers are further described in the next three sections.

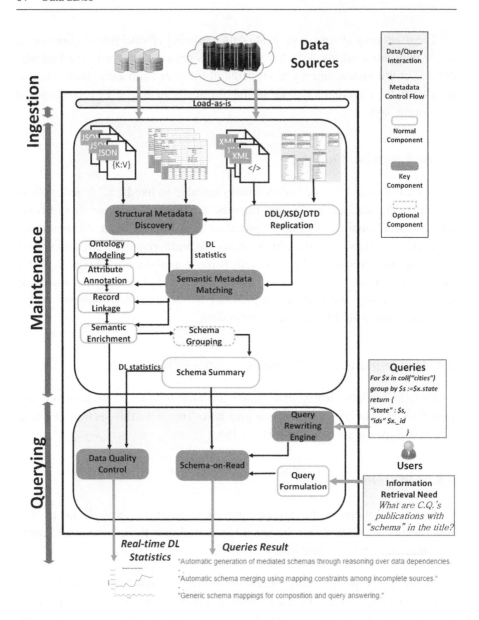

Figure 2.3. *Constance system overview*

2.4.2. *Ingestion layer*

The ingestion layer is responsible for importing data from heterogeneous sources into the data lake system. Different from the traditional E.T.L. process, Constance loads data in their original format without forcing expensive transformation or integration tasks. As shown in Figure 2.3, regardless of the format of the source data (e.g. JSON, spreadsheets, XML or relational data), data are loaded and stored in Constance in their original format.

Notably, for further metadata processing in the maintenance layer of the system, Constance extracts metadata from the data sources into a unified metamodel.

2.4.3. *Maintenance layer*

The components in this layer mainly contribute to the management of metadata, which is crucial for future querying. The backend of the maintenance layer provides the basic functions for data storage and efficient querying. The first step of metadata management is extracting as much metadata as possible from the sources.

For relational tables and some XML documents, explicit schema definitions (in SQL, XSD, or DTD) can be directly obtained from the source and integrated into the metamodel. The tricky part is semi-structured data (such as XML without XSD, JSON), or partially structured Excel or CSV files that contain implicit schemas. The *Structural Metadata Discovery* (SMD) component takes over the responsibility of discovering implicit metadata (e.g. entity types relationship types and constraints) from semi-structured data in a two-fold manner:

1) The SMD checks whether metadata is encoded inside the raw data file, in the filename, or the directories of the file system. An example is the self-describing spreadsheet in Figure 2.3, from which SMD extracts the schema (headers in columns and rows).

2) For semi-structured documents such as JSON or XML, SMD discovers "Has-a"-relationships and stores them in a path-like structure. Notably, as JSON records may not have sufficient relationships among documents, during run time, Constance calculates frequencies of the entities which

appeared in join conditions of user queries, marks them as potential foreign key relationships, and builds indexes accordingly in order to improve the performance.

This part is referred to as *incrementally maturing of a data lake*, as the metadata will be enriched in a "pay-as-you-go" fashion while users are using the system.

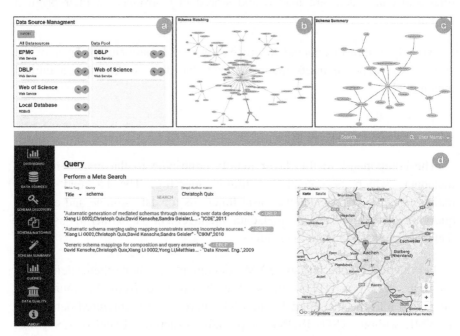

Figure 2.4. *Major components of Constance user interface: (a) data source management, (b) schema matching, (c) schema summary, (d) query answering*

Another key component of this layer is the *Semantic Metadata Matching* (SMM) component, which consists of ontology modeling, attribute annotation, record linkage and semantic enrichment. As can be seen in Figure 2.4(b), the output of this component is a graph representation of the extracted metadata elements and their relationships. Semantic annotations about the meaning of some metadata items can be added to schema elements, and therefore, can be exploited for querying. These semantic annotations are usually performed based on standardized domain-specific models or ontologies, which provides a common, shared understanding of the domain.

Using the semantic annotations, it is possible to perform a first shallow integration of the data as metadata elements with different labels (e.g. attributes "dob" and "DateOfBirth") can be linked if they are annotated with the same semantic element (e.g. "foaf:birthday"). The user can then use the semantic term "foaf:birthday" in a query; the query rewriting module of Constance rewrites the user query into a union of queries which use the schema elements from the sources.

As an optional step, called *Schema Grouping*, clusters the schemas and picks up the core of each cluster as its presentation. The necessity of grouping depends on the schema similarity calculated over the imported data sources. If the schemas are very distinctive or almost the same, schema grouping would not contribute much to the overall system improvement.

Based on the enriched and potentially grouped metadata, the *Schema Summary* component extracts a further compact structure of the currently managed schemata, which we refer to as a *skeleton* [WAN 15], as sketched in Figure 2.4.c. Summarizing schemata is a method of filtering the most important elements or relationships, respectively, within a complex schema. Elements and relationships used more frequently in instance data or queries are considered as more important.

2.4.4. *Query layer*

All the above-mentioned functions possibly serve for information retrieval, in the form of query answering. In common cases, users either input queries in a particular query language, or they have an information retrieval interface which supports them in formulating a query based on some keywords. Depending on these two ways to express queries, Constance distributes the user requirements either to the *Query Rewriting Engine* or to the *Query Formulation* component.

Constance currently implements a query language which is a subset of JSONiq (a query language for JSON-based systems which is similar to XQuery [FLO 13]) as this language enables the easy querying of semi-structured data in JSON. The semantic annotations mentioned above can be seen as simple global-as-view mappings, which means that a single user query might be rewritten into a union of queries over the sources in which the semantic terms are replaced with the original schema elements of the sources.

We are currently working on more complex mappings and query languages, based on our previous work on second-order tuple generating dependencies for mappings between generic data models [KEN 09].

In the case where the user prefers to use keywords, the *Query Formulation* component provides support in creating formal queries that express the intended information requirement. The user will only see a simple natural language representation of the query. The entered values will be matched with metadata and data values. Depending on the matched items, the system will propose further related (meta)data items (e.g. if "publication" has been recognized, the system might propose "author" and "title"). The goal is to have in the end a formal query expressed in the JSONiq-subset.

2.4.5. *Data quality control*

Additionally to the advanced metadata management and querying functions, Constance also provides means for data quality management.

The data quality model is based on our previous works for data warehouses [JAR 99] and data streams [GEI 11]. We define quality factors based on metrics which perform data quality measurements by executing queries (which return some aggregate values) or by invoking some specific functions (implemented as Java methods). The definition of quality metrics is application-specific and can be defined by the user for their data lake instance. The values are presented in a summarized form in a data quality dashboard.

2.4.6. *Extensibility and flexibility*

So far, we have introduced the generic components of Constance. To apply it in real-life projects, scenario-specific functionalities have to be integrated. Mostly notably in the raw data ingestion, the extractor components have to be adapted to some concrete data sources. We have developed an extensible and flexible framework for the ingestion phase in which the existing generic extractors can be adapted to new data source formats (e.g. by providing patterns for the data to be extracted from CSV or Excel files) or new extractors can be easily added using a plug-in mechanism.

On the querying side, the users might expect special ways of data visualization or data interaction of the query results. For example, as indicated in Figure 2.4.d., fields referring to a geographic location (in this case, the author's affiliation) may be visualized in a map.

2.5. Concluding remarks

The main challenge is to keep the flexibility of the original idea of a data lake, whilst making sure that the data lake is not used as a dumping ground for any kind of data garbage.

This requires some governance and quality control, the specification of minimum requirements for data to be put into the data lake. Most publications agree that metadata management is a crucial component in a data lake system, but lack a detailed description of their required functionalities. Moreover, since problems caused by data heterogeneity are currently mostly solved by very *ad hoc* solutions, further research is needed at the levels of query rewriting, data transformation and query optimization.

Nevertheless, the lazy, "pay-as-you-go" principle of a data lake might simplify the implementation of an integration system. It is important to note that many techniques have to be adapted to take into account the incremental and flexible nature of the data lake approach.

3

Exploiting Software Product Lines and Formal Concept Analysis for the Design of Data Lake Architectures

The main objective of this work is to investigate an approach to assisting the user in the design of a data lake architecture. This work can thus be seen as a step, in a more global strategy, towards the development of architectures of information systems, given a specific domain.

Software product line engineering is an approach that allows for the formalization of a series of similar software products or systems, which only differ in some of their optional components. When dealing with data lakes, this approach is independent from softwares, but takes into account the main components or features that have been identified in Chapter 1. Consequently, the obtained formalization allows for significant gains in terms of costs, processing time and quality.

3.1. Our expectations

It is important to recall that the concept of data lake originates from, on the one hand, the need to deal with massive volumes of data and, on the other hand, the use of Apache Hadoop technology. As seen in the previous two

---

Chapter written by Marianne HUCHARD, Anne LAURENT, Thérèse LIBOUREL, Cédrine MADERA and André MIRALLES.

chapters, the association between data lake and Apache Hadoop technology is restrictive and did not really meet users expectations. This explains why data lake architecture has evolved towards hybrid architectures.

Considering that, in many cases, applications are not isolated systems independent from each other, but rather share needs, functionalities and properties, the main idea behind software product lines is to exploit these common features, in order to design an architecture, based on which, other applications can be easily built up.

Until now, very few research works has been devoted to formalizing data lakes. In industry, people have identified the need for data lakes and proposed software solutions accordingly, but these people did not investigate theoretical issues about the formalization of data lakes [IBM 14].

To address this issue, we introduce the concept of software product lines for data lakes, with the goal of formalizing data lakes and assessing the relevance of our approach. Our expectations are thus:

1) to propose a list of components necessary for the settlement of a data lake, while preventing it from being transformed into a swamp;

2) to pave the way for formalizing the concept of data lake.

As for the first item above, given a software product line, our goal is to distinguish which features are common to all products in the line, from the features that might differ from one product to the other. Such a distinction is known as the *feature model* (FM) [CAR 18]. FMs thus model common expectations and those that might differ among all products in the line. FMs are used in many tasks in software product line management, mainly in tasks dealing with information representation, and also in tasks related to the design or the identification of products in a given line, or even in tasks defining the way this line changes and is maintained.

For example, FMs can allow for the identification of compulsory functionalities and of optional ones. This would then facilitate the design the architecture of the various components of a data lake. Figure 3.1 shows the FM obtained in our own work regarding the categorization functionality.

To obtain such FM, we rely on our practical knowledge in industry and our experience in building data lakes, so as to identify the knowledge necessary to design a software product line. To this end, a repository of all features of a data lake has to be created, as described in the next section.

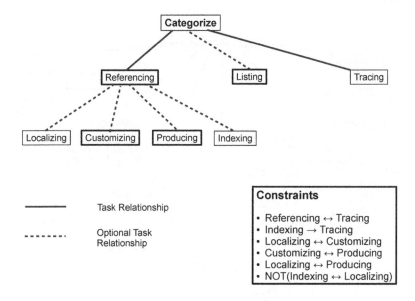

Figure 3.1. *Feature model of the categorization functionality*

3.2. Modeling data lake functionalities

In order to produce a repository of data lake functionalities, we recall from Chapter 1 that data lake functionalities should address the following issues: data acquisition, metadata catalog, data storage, data exploration, data governance, data lifecycle and data quality.

For each of these issues, we have identified all related tasks that have been modeled, as shown in Figure 3.2. In doing so, we could identify the following six basic functionalities:

– acquisition;

– categorization;

– lifecycle management;

– exploitation;

– securing;

– storage.

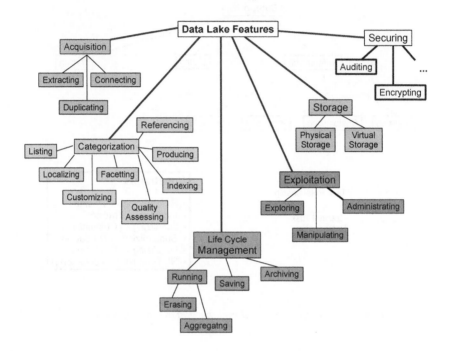

Figure 3.2. *Modeling a data lake through functionalities. For a color version of this figure, see www.iste.co.uk/laurent/data.zip*

In our work, these functionalities are considered basic but non exhaustive, and we rely on them for the construction of our repository. For each functionality, we have identified the related tasks, based on the literature, which is quite poor regarding this issue [ALR 15, CAS 16, FAN 15, HAI 16, MAD 16, MIL 16], as well as on various use cases from industry [RUS 17, IBM 14]. These tasks can be seen as functionalities and can have several variants that are seen as sub tasks and thus as some refined functionalities. It is therefore necessary to develop a formal method for modeling features.

To illustrate our approach in the case of the *acquisition* functionality, we have first distinguished structured data from unstructured data, whereas semi-structured data were not considered at this level. For each category, it has been found that all related tasks are quite similar at the modeling level, but that they differ on the techniques used to achieve these tasks in the data lake.

We have also made a distinction between real-time processing and batch processing. Note that we also could have considered the three possible ways of data acquisition, as mentioned in [MIL 16] (i.e. batch, real-time and hybrid), but this was not considered relevant. As mentioned previously, the related tasks were found quite similar when considering the two types of processing, differing on the techniques used to achieve them in the data lake.

Based on this work, the following main tasks were identified: *extract*, *duplicate* and *connect*, and this has been the basis for building our first repository regarding the *acquisition* functionality.

Doing a similar work for all other basic functionalities, we came up with the following tasks for each of them:

– *Categorization:* listing, typing, referencing, localizing, customizing, producing, indexing, listing the facets, quality assessing, tracing.

– *Lifecycle management:* running, erasing, erasing for technical reasons, aggregating, summarizing, saving, archiving.

– *Exploitation:* preparing, enriching, aggregating, labeling, pattern recognition, classifying, cleaning, reconciling, correlating, transforming, exploring/producing, navigating, describing, computing statistics patterns or rules, reporting, segmenting, predicting, prescribing, inferring, querying, releasing, managing.

– *Securing:* protecting, encrypting, managing confidentiality, anonymizing, auditing, complying.

– *Storage:* physically storing, virtually storing.

Once this experimental repository was built, we proceeded to set up a knowledge base.

3.3. Building the knowledge base of industrial data lakes

We studied six use cases of industrial data lakes, based on our repository, and for each of them, we identified all functionalities and associated tasks performed in the data lake.

To this end, spreadsheets were built up, as shown in Figure 3.3, for the acquisition functionality[1]. For instance, it can be seen from Figure 3.3 that Client 5 has all functionalities but 4, and that Acquerir/Donnees Structurees/Extraire (Collect/Structured Data/Extract) has been chosen by all clients.

					Client 1	Client 2	Client 3.i	Client 3.n	Client 4	Client 5	Client 6
Acquérir					x	x	x	x	x	x	x
	Données structurées				x	x	x	x	x	x	x
		Extraire			x	x	x	x	x	x	x
			Initial		x	x	x	x	x	x	x
				Temps réel							
				Temps différé	x	x	x	x	x	x	x
			Courant		x	x	x	x		x	x
				Temps réel	x	x	x	x		x	x
				Temps différé	x	x	x	x			x
		Dupliquer			x	x	x	x	x	x	x
			Initial		x	x	x	x	x	x	x
				Temps réel						x	x
				Temps différé	x	x	x	x	x	x	x
			Courant		x	x	x	x		x	x
				Temps réel			x			x	x
				Temps différé	x	x	x	x		x	x
		Connecter (flux)			x	x			x	x	
			Initial			x			x	x	
				Temps réel		x			x		
				Temps différé					x	x	
			Courant		x	x				x	
				Temps réel		x				x	
				Temps différé	x					x	
	Données non structurées				x	x			x		
		Extraire				x			x	x	
			Initial			x			x	x	
				Temps réel						x	
				Temps différé		x			x	x	
			Courant			x				x	
				Temps réel		x				x	
				Temps différé		x				x	
		Dupliquer			x	x			x	x	
			Initial		x	x			x	x	
				Temps réel					x	x	
				Temps différé	x	x			x	x	
			Courant		x	x				x	
				Temps réel	x					x	
				Temps différé	x	x				x	
		Connecter			x	x				x	
			Initial			x				x	
				Temps réel		x				x	
				Temps différé						x	
			Courant		x	x				x	
				Temps réel	x	x				x	
				Temps différé						x	

Figure 3.3. *Knowledge base - acquisition functionality*

---

1 As this was addressed to French users, the spreadsheet is presented in its original form, in French.

Having built a repository for data lake functionalities, we introduce our formalization approach based on the model of product lines in the next section.

Before doing so, we recall basic notions and terminology related to *Software Product Line* and *Formal Concept Analysis*.

We rely on the work by Clements and Northrop [CLE 01], in which the concept of software product line is defined as follows:

> *Software product line is a set of software-intensive systems sharing a common, managed set of features that satisfy the specific need of a particular market segment or mission and that are developed from a common set of core assets in a prescribed way.*

As for terminology, our guideline in this respect is based on a survey by J. Cabonnel and M. Huchard [CAR 18]) as summarized below.

Formal concept analysis (FCA): according to [GAN 99], FCA can be defined as a formalism for structuring a set of objects described by attributes. A formal concept describes a binary relation between objects and attributes meaning that "object O has attribute A" (see Figure 3.8). Based on a formal context, an FCA allows for the extraction of an *ordered* set of concepts.

Concept: a concept is a maximum set of objects sharing a maximum set of attributes by means of the relation between objects and attributes of the corresponding formal concept. Figure 3.4 shows a concept related to the storage functionality.

Concept lattice: we recall that a *lattice* is a partially ordered set in which every non-empty subset has a unique maximum element and a unique minimum element. It can be shown that the set of all concepts in a given formal concept can be equipped with a partial ordering so as to form a lattice called *concept lattice*. Figure 3.5 shows the concept lattice composed of three concepts regarding storage functionality, ordered according to the specific relation explained in the figure.

Equivalence class feature diagram (ECFD): an ECFD is a set of logical relations built up from the description of variants in a given feature model (FM). ECFDs can be seen as a normalized form that provides a unique representation of variability throughout several FMs. Figure 3.6 shows one of the ECFDs that were built up in our work regarding the categorization functionality and some of its associated tasks and their constraints, as shown in Figure 3.1.

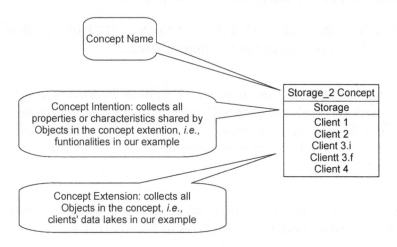

Figure 3.4. *A concept*

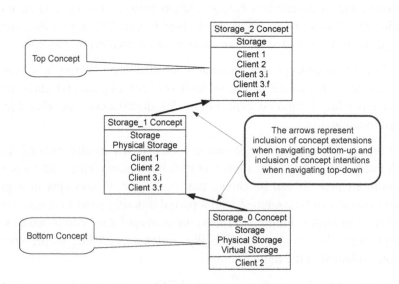

Figure 3.5. *A concept lattice*

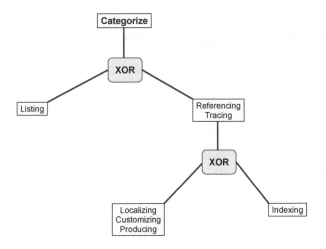

Figure 3.6. *An equivalent class feature diagram*

3.4. Our formalization approach

We considered the following steps in our approach:

– formal context generation;

– production of the corresponding FCA;

– construction of a concept lattice and its simplified version;

– automatic composition of the associated ECFD;

– manual construction of the corresponding FM.

This methodology has been applied for the tables derived from our knowledge base.

During the construction of the knowledge base, two different ways were considered: one regarding functionalities and one regarding software components. However, it should be noted that only the former way was subsequently used in our experiments, whereas it is planned to use the latter in our future work.

Then, we have identified six main functionalities, so as to produce easy-to-read FMs. We recall from section 3.2 that these functionalities are: acquisition, categorization, lifecycle management, exploitation, securing and storage. In doing so, we obtained six entry-points for our approach to software product line.

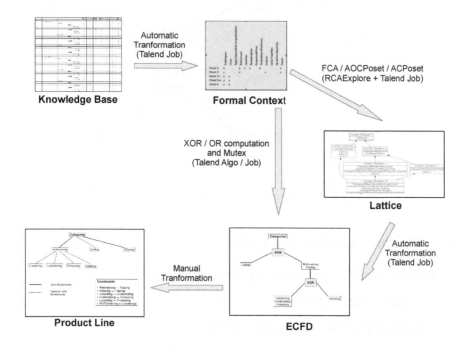

Figure 3.7. *Our process for the production of product lines*

The following remarks should be made regarding our work.

1) We first mention that we used an existing semi-automatic process, as shown in Figure 3.7.

2) Moreover, it should be emphasized that the knowledge base evolves through time. In particular, it is continuously enriched with new collaborations. In this respect, we emphasize that, when starting this work, only four functionalities were considered, and then two other functionalities came in. Through this enrichment, we could observe that FMs were evolving, but we did not precisely analyze the evolution.

3) It can be considered that the number of cases, when building our knowledge base, is quite low, thus implying that the interpretations of concept

lattices are debatable. In this respect, we note that in order to compensate for this lack of data, our results were systematically validated by experts.

3.5. Applying our approach

Thanks to the semi-automatic process and our knowledge base, we could generate all formal contexts associated with each of the six functionalities identified earlier. Figure 3.8[2] shows the context of *categorization* functionality for every industrial case, and a similar representation has been produced for the other five functionalities.

				Client 1	Client 2	Client 3.i	Client 3.n	Client 4	Client 5	Client 6
Cataloguer				x	x	x	x	x	x	x
	Lister					x	x	x	x	x
	Typer (sensiblité en particulier)								x	x
	Référencer			x	x				x	x
		Localiser		x						
		Personnaliser		x					x	x
			Responsabiliser						x	x
			Production (Produire)	x					x	
		Indexer			x				x	
	Lister Facettes									
	Qualifier (Qualité)								x	x
	Tracer			x	x					x

	cataloguer	Lister	typer	referencer	localiser	personnaliser	responsabiliser	produire	Indexer	lister	qualifier	tracer
Client 1	X			X	X	x		x				x
Client 2	X			X					X			X
Client 3.i	X	X										
Client 3.n	X	X										
Client 4	X	X										
Client 5	X	X	X	X		X	X	X	X		X	
Client 6	X	X	X	X								X

Figure 3.8. *Creation of the formal context for the categorization functionality*

---

2 The displayed spreadsheets are those that have effectively been produced and processed. This explains why they are in French.

Based on this formal context, we could process some formal concept analyses which yielded concept lattices. Figure 3.9 shows one such concept lattice associated with the *secure* functionality and its associated formal context.

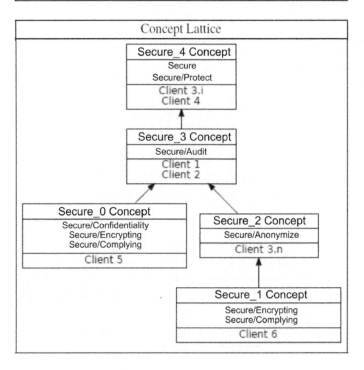

		1 yr	2 yrs	2 yrs	3 mos.	3 yrs	3 yrs	3 yrs
				Intitial version	Current version			
		DL 1	DL 2	DL 3i	DL 3f	DL 4	DL 5	DL 6
		Client 1	Client 2	Client 3.i	Client 3.n	Client 4	Client 5	Client 6
Secure		x	x	x	x	x	x	x
	Protect	x	x	x	x	x	x	x
	Encrypting						x	x
	Confidentiality						x	
	Anonymize				x			x
	Audit	x	x		x		x	x
	Complying						x	x

Figure 3.9. *Formal context and the associated concept in the case of secure functionality*

Using three different types of algorithms, we could generate different concept lattices, each of them delivering different but complementary information. This step being automated, in each case, lattices were produced in two forms, simplified and complete. We thus obtained six types of lattices per functionality: AFC, AC-poset and AOC-poset. We refer to Figures 3.9 and 3.10 for an illustration of these types of lattices in the case of the secure functionality. For instance, it can be seen from Figure 3.9 that Client 3.i and Client 4 are the only clients with the concepts secure and secure/protect (and no other concept). Moreover, Client 3.n is the only client with the following four concepts: secure/anonymize, secure/audit, secure and secure/protect, these four concepts being obtained by unioning all concepts from this box to the top one ($\{Secure/Anonymize\} \cup \{Secure/Audit\} \cup \{Secure, Secure/Protect\}$).

For every functionality, considering the formal context and its associated concept lattice, the ETL tool Talend has been used for generating the corresponding ECFD (see Figure 3.7). In Figure 3.6, we show how the ECFD has been obtained in the case of *categorization* functionality.

Then, FMs were obtained through a manual process (see Figure 3.1 in the case of *categorization* functionality). It is important to note that this step cannot be automatized because an expert is required for checking the consistency of the output. Moreover, the associated expert rules have not been stated yet.

Summing up our approach, we could set up a semi-automatic process that uses existing tools for software product lines, in order to generate an FM for each functionality of a data lake.

3.6. Analysis of our first results

We analyzed all FMs and associated concept lattices in order to have an indication on the maturity of settling the industrial cases used in the construction of our knowledge base.

This analysis has led us to design a questionnaire on the maturity of data lakes and on the prevention of data lakes becoming swamps when omitting some tasks associated with functionalities. This questionnaire has been applied to two new industrial cases which will be used in order to enrich our knowledge base and thus improve our future analyses.

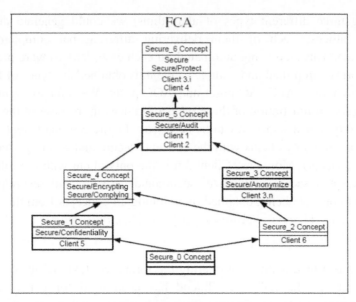

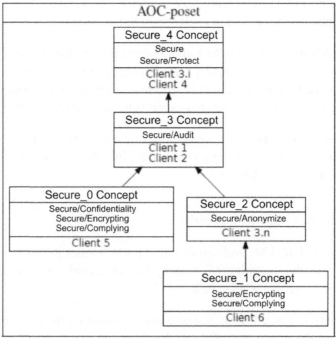

Figure 3.10. *The FCA and AOC-poset for the secure functionality*

To illustrate the way our questionnaire is built up, some questions regarding the *acquisition* functionality are listed as follows:

– Are data on data sources listed?

– Using which tool? Under which form (database, metadata catalog, etc.)?

– Are data on data sources typed (in particular regarding sensibility)?

– Are data on data sources referenced? Localized? Personalized?

– Is there any tool for managing master data in the data lake or out of the data lake?

– Is there any data stewardship for the management of data and data sources?

– Is there anybody responsible for the production of data on data sources?

– Are the data on data sources indexed or tagged?

– Are the data on data sources faceted (i.e. are these data always associated with a "point of view")?

– Are the data on data sources qualified regarding their quality?

– Are the data on data sources associated with their lineage?

– Is there a tool and a base for the management of metadata?

3.7. Concluding remarks

In this chapter, we have shown an approach to assisting and accelerating the construction of a data lake. This approach consists of high-level modeling, independent from physical tools, relying on existing software product line concepts.

In order to assess our approach, we have built a repository of data lake functionalities and then created a knowledge base for data lakes, based on our previous experiments and collaborations in industry. With this knowledge base at hand, we were able to use existing semi-automated processes to generate the feature model (FM) that provides us with a preliminary formal model regarding the functionalities of the components of a data lake.

An analysis of our preliminary results allowed us to design a questionnaire for the evaluation of the maturity of data lakes and of the prevention of them becoming swamps. This analysis shows that our approach is relevant, even though it still has to be refined in collaboration with experts in software product line management.

4

Metadata in Data Lake Ecosystems

The notion of metadata has been used in information management long before the emergence of computer science, in fields related to documentation or cataloguing. In fact, this notion was first introduced in Greek libraries for storing and classifying manuscripts, based on descriptive tags [MFI 17].

Organizing information resources (i.e. objects in the real world, data, abstract concepts, services, etc.) has been the main motivation of describing, structuring and documenting them with metadata. According to the National Information Security Organization (NISO) [RIL 17], metadata have been shown to be relevant in data management because they provide data sources with a context, allowing users to understand the data in the short, medium or long term.

In this chapter, the following issues are addressed: what are metadata? What has been done in this field? Is metadata useful for data lakes?

4.1. Definitions and concepts

According to NISO [RIL 17], the notion of metadata is defined as structured information for describing, explaining, localizing and aiding the retrieval, use or management of an information resource. Metadata is often called "data about data" or "information about information".

Chapter written by Asma ZGOLLI, Christine COLLET† and Cédrine MADERA.

According to "Open Data Support", metadata provide information giving some meaning to data (documents, images, datasets), concepts (e.g. classification schema) or real-world entities (e.g. people, organizations, locations, masterpieces, products) [DAL 13].

4.2. Classification of metadata by NISO

The NISO classification of metadata encompasses the following four types:

– *Descriptive metadata*: the purpose of these metadata is to ease information retrieval or discovery. Examples of this type of metadata are the name of the author of a book, annotations or abstracts.

– *Structural metadata*: these metadata are used for the description of the schema of data. Examples of this type of metadata are the definition of types, attributes and constraints.

– *Administrative metadata*: these metadata are low-level metadata, such as the size of data and the date of creation or modification. This type has the following three subtypes:

  - technical metadata, used for decoding and displaying the data (considering that data are stored in files),

  - preservation metadata, used for the long term file management,

  - rights metadata, used for legacy issues such as copyrights or intellectual property.

– *Markup languages* (e.g. HTML) that allow for the storage of metadata and of flags for further features about the structure of the semantics of the data.

Table 4.1 summarizes the examples given by NISO about the different types of metadata [RIL 17].

Metadata type	Example properties	Primary uses
Descriptive metadata	Title Author Subject Type Publication date	Discovery Display Interoperability
Technical metadata	File type File size Creation data/time Compression schema	Interoperability Digital object management Preservation
Preservation metadata	Checksum Preservation event	Interoperability Digital object management Preservation
Rights metadata	Copyright status License terms Rights holder	Interoperability Digital object management
Structural metadata	Sequence Place in hierarchy	Navigation
Markup languages	Paragraph Heading List Name Date	Navigation Interoperability

Table 4.1. *Metadata classification by NISO [RIL 17]*

4.2.1. *Metadata schema*

A metadata schema consists of a labeling, marking or encoding system, used for storing information about the way data is organized and structured. It is used to state the concepts and rules that define how to use the data for describing a resource. Standard metadata schemas have been proposed in order to define generic types to be shared and used in many projects. The most popular norms for metadata schemas are the following [RIL 17]:

1) Dublin core (http://dublincore.org/documents/dcmi-terms/). This standard was developed for describing resources to be mined. It is used to provide information about web pages and can be used in browsers.

2) FOAF (Friend Of A Friend, http://xmlns.com/foaf/spec/). This standard is for describing people, their activity and their relationships with other people or objects. FOAF is, for example, widely used for modeling social networks.

3) SKOS (Simple Knowledge Organization Systems, http://www.w3. org/TR/skos-reference/). Citing the abstract of the website given above, this standard is defined as a *"common data model for sharing and linking knowledge organization systems via the Web"*. More precisely, and partly paraphrasing the abstract just mentioned, SKOS captures many similarities between organization systems, such as thesauri, taxonomies, classification schemes and subject heading systems.

4) DCAT (Data Catalog Vocabulary, http://www.w3.org/TR/vovab-dcat/). Citing the abstract of the website given above:

> DCAT is an RDF vocabulary designed to facilitate interoperability between data catalogs published on the Web. By using DCAT to describe datasets in data catalogs, publishers increase discoverability and enable applications easily to consume metadata from multiple catalogs. It further enables decentralized publishing of catalogs and facilitates federated dataset search across sites. Aggregated DCAT metadata can serve as a manifest file to facilitate digital preservation.

4.2.2. *Knowledge base and catalog*

As defined in [WIK 16], "A knowledge base (KB) is a technology used to store complex structured and unstructured information used by a computer system." Knowledge bases are of various kinds, among which we cite rule-based systems and knowledge network systems. Despite their diversity, all knowledge bases aim at the same target, namely gathering expertise of the given domain and exploiting it through and inference engine [TEA 18c].

On the other hand, a data catalog is a data structure equipped with a service for accessing data sources described in the catalog. A data catalog can contain metadata, such as definitions of objects in the associated database (tables, views, index or annotations). The features associated with a data catalog thus allow users to share their knowledge [FER 15, TEA 17].

4.3. Other categories of metadata

Other categories of metadata are also used in some organizations, namely[1]:

– business metadata;

– navigational metadata;

– operational metadata.

4.3.1. *Business metadata*

Business metadata define the information content that the data provide in a business context. This includes the information needed to support data understanding and use by the end user. Examples of business metadata, are business entity and attribute names, business entity and attribute definitions, business attribute sub-values, data quality rules, semantic data models, relationships and business terms associated with applications.

Business metadata are an important aspect in any successful information governance program. For example, in the data stewardship process, supporting business metadata can include steward contact information, steward-owned business terms, business term status and so on. Additionally, business metadata frequently includes business process metadata, describing processes and their characteristics. Business metadata are produced by processes that create logical data models, data quality criteria workbooks, business intelligence (BI) reports and data stewardship processes. They are also produced by business process design and management - business process management (BPM), business services, business rules and business applications.

Business metadata should be available for all technical or business resources. Important users of business metadata include auditors, BI users who create reports and queries, data analysts, financial analysts, managers, data stewards and data owners. Business metadata are also used by system development staff such as data architects, application database administrators,

---

1 From **IBM** Information governance view: http://www.redbooks.ibm.com/redbooks/pdfs/sg 247939.pdf.

data integration analysts, data integration architects and data integration developers.

Business rules: each business rule must be one of the following:

– a *structural assertion*, a defined concept or a statement of a fact expressing some aspect of the structure of an enterprise. This encompasses both terms and the facts assembled based on these terms;

– an *action assertion*, a statement of a constraint or condition that limits or controls the actions of the enterprise;

– a *derivation*, a statement of knowledge that is derived from other knowledge in the business.

A *structural assertion* is a statement that something of importance to the business either exists as a concept of interest, or exists in relationship to another thing of interest. It details a specific, static aspect of the business, expressing things that are known or how known things fit together. Structural assertions are frequently portrayed by entity/relationship models. There are two kinds: terms and facts (facts relating to one or more terms).

An *action assertion* is a statement that concerns some dynamic aspect of the business and is directly associated with a business rule. It specifies constraints on the results that actions can produce. The constraints are described in a non-procedural way, in terms of the other atomic business rules. While structural assertions describe possibilities, action assertions impose constraints.

A *derived fact* is created by an inference or a mathematical calculation from terms, facts, other derivations, or even action assertions. Each derived fact must be derived using one derivation. The derivation, in turn, must be based on one or more business rules. In other words, a *derivation* must also be used to derive at least one and possibly more derived facts.

Primary sources of structural metadata are database catalogs, physical data models, application and server import files. The primary audience for structural metadata are database administrators (DBAs), programmers, data architects, data integration analysts, data integration architects and data integration developers. They also provide value to data analysts, data modelers and data stewards.

4.3.2. *Navigational integration*

Navigational integration metadata describe the data linkage and data movement within the environments. They represent the integration of the data: the ETL (extract, transform and load) processing information. Examples of navigational integration metadata are derived attributes, business hierarchies, source columns/fields, transformations, data quality checkpoints, target columns/fields and source/target locations.

Data quality checks and valid value look-ups are examples of data integration rules. A data integration rule includes information about where data comes from, how it is extracted, transformed and where it is landed. This type of navigational/integration metadata supports data lineage and impact analysis.

Navigational integration metadata also includes information about business analytics lineage; in other words, data lineage to reporting. Examples are report name, report field name, report field definition and so on. Primary sources of structural metadata include logical/physical data integration models, data quality criteria workbooks and business analytics imports.

The primary audiences for navigational integration metadata are data integration analysts, data integration architects, data integration developers and data stewards. It also provides value to data architects, data analysts and data modelers.

4.3.3. *Operational metadata*

Operational metadata describes the data integration applications and supporting job runs. These applications and jobs involve handling functions that capture, store, maintain and distribute data. To effectively control these functions, metadata related to their operation must be gathered and reported. Examples of operational metadata include job statistics, job status, frequency and data quality check results (e.g. record counts).

Primary sources of operational metadata include data integration job logs and data quality checks. The primary audiences for operational metadata are the production support, system operations, system administrators, network administrators, data integration analysts, data integration developers and data integration architects. It also provides value to data architects, data stewards and data analysts. Operational metadata assists by giving these resources the ability to track the processing of data across systems, ultimately assisting them in troubleshooting data or data quality problems.

4.4. Sources of metadata

Metadata produced in-house by human beings is probably what most people assume when they think of a metadata source. This is metadata created manually by the specialist cataloger, subject expert or volunteer. The cost of this is high but it is also, usually, the most important metadata, especially to the end user.

Historically, metadata was primarily focused on describing data held in relational databases and data warehouses. Document management systems also contained a lot of metadata, but typically it was located within the document management system for purposes of locating and managing the documents. Today, sources of metadata are much wider and include:

– other varieties of data stores: NoSQL (key-value and document-based typically have very little metadata), graph, object;

– unorganized document management systems (network file share);

– unstructured media (video, image, audio);

– digital (web logs, mobile);

– IoT, sensors, wearables;

– external sources, B2B, social media;

– machine learning, cognitive, artificial intelligence.

Crowdsourcing metadata are metadata collected for free by organizations from their audience to help describing and commenting resources. The most common example of crowdsourced metadata takes the form of tags and keywords. Users may be asked for more on context and use cases. Gamification may be used to increase participation.

4.5. Metadata classification

Different purposes benefit from different types of metadata. Business users use metadata to understand the available data and the possible conclusions the data may support. Technical users need metadata to develop systems that can deliver high quality data. Metadata may support different kinds of initiatives, including data warehousing and business intelligence projects, system integration projects, infrastructure support efforts, enterprise architecture initiatives, as well as being the key to information governance.

Metadata management seeks to provide business and technical users with easier access to integrated, high quality metadata. However, because there are so many different types of metadata, trying to manage all types of metadata at once will lead only to frustration, exhausting efforts without satisfying needs. Therefore, organizations should prioritize different types of metadata, focusing efforts to successfully manage the types of metadata needed to support critical business needs.

The subject area model shown in Figure 4.1 defines 16 different subject areas that might be chosen for inclusion in an enterprise metadata repository. Several of these subject areas are *core* subject areas that describe data and its use, and are more commonly found within an integrated metadata repository.

Data structure metadata: this involves data about physical files, relational database tables and columns, indexes and other database control objects. Data structure metadata are specifications within physical designs for data structures in development, test or production. This metadata also includes data about usage, performance and change management. Data structure metadata may describe transactional databases, data warehouses or data marts. For relational databases, the definitive source for data structure metadata is the relational database management system catalog. Until implemented, the best alternative sources are the Data Definition Language (DDL) specifications or the physical design model created using a data modeling tool. Some examples of sources are Xml, Json and COBOL copybooks.

While most metadata in this subject area is navigational metadata (describing technical names, lengths and physical data types), the subject area also includes business name equivalents for these technical table and column names and their business definitions. The data structure metadata subject area is the most widely used. The meta models for virtually all metadata repository tools support this central, primary subject area.

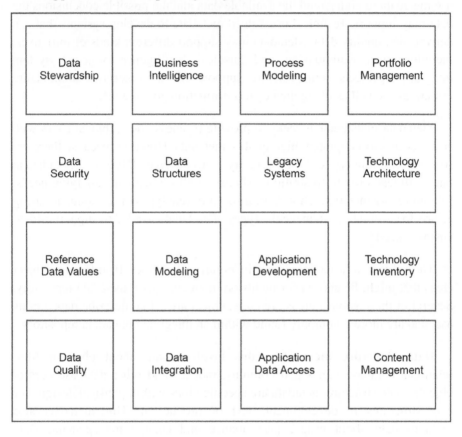

Figure 4.1. *Metadata subject areas*

Data modeling metadata: this involves data about business entities, their attributes, subject areas, relationships between entities and business rules governing these relationships. Data modeling metadata includes business names and business definitions for these entities and attributes. This metadata defines the cells in rows 1–3 of column 1 in the Zachman framework.

The definitive sources for data modeling metadata are the conceptual and logical data models created using data modeling tools. The data modeling metadata subject area also includes metadata that relates equivalent data entities and attributes across different data models and relate these models to metadata in the data structure metadata subject area, describing the physical implementation of conceptual and logical data models. These *linkage metadata* may be recorded in extensions to data models or entered independently into the metadata repository once the metadata from each data model have been extracted and loaded into the metadata repository.

Data stewardship metadata: this involves data about data stewards, information governance organizations, data steward responsibility assignments for data modeling metadata about subject areas, business entities and/or attributes, and data steward responsibility assignments for the quality of data in databases, relational tables and columns. This metadata may be entered directly into a metadata repository or loaded from other sources.

Data integration metadata: this involves data about the mappings and transformations (and therefore the business rules) used in Extract-Transform-Load (ETL) programs to migrate data from the source to the target. This metadata may also be sourced from enterprise application interface (EAI) tools and enterprise information integration (EII) tools that perform transformations on the data.

Business intelligence metadata: this involves data about business intelligence views and interfaces, queries, reports and usage. The metadata in this subject area is sourced from business intelligence tools and is related to data structure metadata, particularly with three-dimensional reporting models. Some subject areas provide other useful data about related aspects of data assets.

Reference value metadata: this involves data about controlled vocabularies and defined domain values, including valid internal and external codes, labels and business meanings. Reference data values appear in transactional data, and business definitions for these values provide context for transactions, transforming this data into meaningful information. Some of this business metadata is sourced from external standards organizations, while other reference data values may be controlled through master data management databases.

Data quality metadata: this involves statistical data about the quality of information, including the number of defects found at given points in time, and summarized to create overall data quality metrics. This subject area is closely linked to the data structure metadata subject area, but the definitive source for this metadata is typically a data quality profiling and analysis tool.

Data security metadata: this involves data about how data access is controlled through security classifications, privileges, users and groups, filters, authentication, security audits and privacy rule compliance.

Application data access metadata: this involves data about how views, queries and application programs access data stored in data structures, and how this data is presented in reports, screens, web pages, XML documents, spreadsheets and flat files, representing inputs to and output deliverables from business processes. The metadata in this subject area is sourced primarily from application program specifications.

Content management metadata: this involves metadata about unstructured data found in documents, including taxonomies, ontologies, XML name sets, search engine keywords, indexes and parameters for legal electronic discovery. The metadata that controls enterprise content management (ECM) may be integrated into a comprehensive enterprise metadata repository.

Other metadata subject areas describe closely related information technology assets (such as application systems, software components and technology infrastructure) and business knowledge assets (such as business processes, organizations, goals and projects), which may also be found within an integrated metadata repository, including the following.

Legacy system metadata: this involves data about legacy application programs and software core modules, the logic defined within the code and their relationships between modules, supporting impact analysis, restructuring, reuse and componentization. The metadata in this subject area is sourced primarily from reverse engineering tools.

Application development metadata: this involves data about application business and technical requirements, application design (including UML specifications), service-oriented architecture (SOA), contemporary application programming objects (Java code, EJB, legacy system wrappers, web services), test plans and test data. Much of this metadata is found within integrated application development environments, design tools, testing tools and software configuration management (SCM) libraries. Some metadata repositories integrate this metadata with metadata from other subject areas and sources for more comprehensive impact analysis, change control and reuse. Much of this metadata may be found in unstructured formats, such as text documents; a structured metadata repository database may be supplemented with a document library for unstructured metadata.

Process modeling metadata: this involves data about processes at any level (including functions, activities, tasks and steps), workflow dependency relationships between processes, business rules, events, roles and responsibilities, and the input–output relationships between processes and deliverables defined in data access metadata. The metadata in this subject area is sourced primarily from process modeling tools. Process modeling metadata is essential to any comprehensive understanding of the enterprise architecture.

Portfolio management metadata: this involves data about goals, objectives, strategies, projects, programs, costs and benefits, organizations, resources, relationships between applications and business processes they support, and alignment of projects with business strategies. This metadata is also an important aspect of the enterprise architecture.

Technology architecture metadata: this involves data about technology standards, including preferred hardware and software products, protocols and configurations.

Technology inventory metadata: this involves data about implemented infrastructure, including hardware, software, networks and their configurations. The metadata in this subject area is often maintained and sourced from system management tools.

The metadata that may be of most value to the enterprise is the metadata connecting these subject areas, defining the relationships between data, processes, applications and technology. This data may not be stored in any traditional metadata source tool but rather may need to be captured separately, perhaps by direct entry into the integrated metadata repository by subject matter experts.

4.6. Why metadata are needed

Metadata constitute a key notion to guarantee that information will survive and continue to be available in the future. Metadata are thus a major asset for enterprises because they improve or allow the following features selection of information resources, organization of information resources, interoperability and integration, unique digital identification, data archiving and protecting [RIL 04, SEL 96]:. More details on each of these features are given next.

4.6.1. *Selection of information (re)sources*

When it comes to searching for or selecting an information source, metadata provide relevant criteria for unambiguously identifying an information resource (e.g. associating data with time stamps allows us to make a choice between different versions of a given information resource) or recognizing and characterizing similar and dissimilar information resources (e.g. associating a photo with GPS coordinates can ease the recognition of similar sources next to each other).

4.6.2. *Organization of information resources*

Metadata can be used for implementing links between information resources based on their use or on their topic. Then, based on such metadata, more characteristics can be stored dynamically in databases (e.g. file profiling).

4.6.3. *Interoperability and integration*

When expressed using interchangeable formats such as XML, RDF or JSON (to cite a few), metadata significantly contribute to defining open systems in which interoperability and integration of data sources are eased in the following ways:

– when using predefined metadata schema, transfer protocols and data exchange interfaces can be searched efficiently through the network;

– searching among various systems can be done using, for example, the Z39.50 protocol (according to Wikipedia, Z39.50 is an "ANSI/NISO international standard client-server, application layer communications protocol for searching and retrieving information from a database over a TCP/IP computer network");

– collecting metadata can be done using, for example, Open Archives Initiative Protocol for Metadata Harvesting (OAI-PMH) (https://www.openarchives.org/pmh/).

4.6.4. *Unique digital identification*

Unique digital identification is achieved by considering as metadata numerical identifiers, such as ISBN (International Standard Book Number) or index on the place where a digital object is stored (e.g. a file name or a URL). Such metadata are either a persistent identifier, such as Persistent URL (PURL) or Digital Object Identifier (DOI), or a combination of persistent metadata that allow for differentiating distinct objects.

4.6.5. *Data archiving and preservation*

Digital information is fragile, as it can be modified or corrupted at any time. Moreover, digital information can become inoperable when storing techniques change. Metadata have been used in this respect for guaranteeing that information resources remain accessible in the future, independently of any corruption or any change of storing technique. Preservation of digital information requires following its lineage, to detail its physical characteristics, in order to reproduce it.

Seen as data, metadata have also to be stored and safely preserved in the system. Moreover, metadata are often created before the actual data, and can be kept after the data have been removed (so as to keep track of the existence of such and such data). Therefore, the lifecycle of metadata is longer than that of "regular data", thus showing the importance of properly storing and protecting metadata.

Many techniques can be used for storing and preserving data and their associated metadata [RIL 04]. These techniques range from standard database XML or RDF systems to NoSQL-specific systems based on graphs.

4.7. Business value of metadata

The 2018 Magic Quadrant from Gartner Group, for Metadata Management Solutions[2], states that "by 2020, 50% of information governance initiatives will be enacted with policies based on metadata alone". This is because metadata provide several very important benefits to the enterprise, including:

Consistency of definitions: metadata contain information about data that helps reconcile the difference in terminology such as *clients*, *customers*, *revenue* and *sales*.

Clarity of relationships: metadata help resolve ambiguity and inconsistencies when determining the associations between entities stored throughout the data environment. For example, if a customer declares a "beneficiary" in one application, and this beneficiary is called a "participant" in another application, metadata definitions would help clarify the situation.

Clarity of data: lineage metadata contain information about the origins of a particular dataset, and can be granular enough to define information at the attribute level; metadata may maintain allowed values for a data attribute, its proper format, location, owner and steward. Tracking data lineage provides important context to business users. Profiling data in source systems by business data stewards and IT staff can resolve data errors, which will result in accurate, reliable, high-quality data presented in reports, queries and analytics.

Clarity of audit information: operationally, metadata may maintain auditable information about users, applications and processes that create, delete or change data, the exact timestamp of the change, and the authorization that was used to perform these actions.

Clarity on privacy: identifiable information metadata can help with data privacy compliance:

– metadata allows easy recording of consent on PII;

– it can provide information on the creation date of the file, the name of the database hacked and when any potential data breach took place;

---

2 https://www.gartner.com/en/documents/3886063.

– metadata can be used to enforce the necessary technical measures required to ensure personal data is only processed for specific purposes that are in line with the overall purpose of the business;

– metadata allows you to easily identify data that is PII when conducting a privacy impact assessment;

– metadata enables fast identification of data locations for data subject access requests.

Improved data discovery: most companies manage increasingly complex systems in various locations and on varied platforms. By managing metadata across the organization, they can simplify data discovery and data heritage with a record of content-rich data.

Reinforced data consistency: reinforcing consistency through data reuse and redundancy elimination allows us to increase productivity and to reduce time needed for project implementation. A managed metadata environment (MME) or other method of managing metadata centrally serves as the most effective way of identifying the appropriate data elements or objects needed for any use. Doing so allows companies to retire unused storage, reduce costs and reduce time that was spent in deciding among *possibly correct* variations of an attribute.

Improved knowledge retention: retaining staff knowledge that is lost when business rules, definitions and other forms of metadata are not documented. Often, business metadata remains only in the minds of certain employees. When these individuals leave the company, this knowledge disappears with them. Implementing an enterprise approach to managing metadata preserves this and reduces the risk of losing valuable contextual knowledge.

Improved IT performance in development: impact analysis, data integration, change management, etc. All of these enhancements will enable greater cooperation between businesses and IT, and ultimately lower total costs of any systems initiative. Metadata helps IT understand what data exists, where it is located and what it means, minimizing information complexity. The ability to assess the impact of potential changes based on improved knowledge of the data can help managers estimate project duration and resource costs more accurately.

Metadata security strategy: an organization can control security down to specific metadata object level by creating role-based profiles, allowing access at a role (rather than individual user) level.

In summary, the implementation of a metadata strategy provides the following business value:

The capability to answer operational and analytical questions about the information gives the:

– knowledge to make accurate, timely, faster informed decisions;

– confidence to take business actions based on the information;

– tools to understand what information he/she is looking at.

That is, it allows the end user to build value through insight.

The metadata strategy enables:

– definition analysis;

– impact analysis;

– where used analysis;

– difference analysis;

– location/navigational analysis;

– data quality analysis.

Metadata provides the metadata user with the capability to answer the following questions:

– What do I have?

– What does it mean?

– How current is it?

– Where did it come from?

– Where does it go?

– How do I get it?

4.8. Metadata architecture

Planning the end-to-end metadata architecture is necessary to identify and understand all integration points. Additionally, knowing what metadata is easy to obtain, load and deploy identifies quick wins. Understanding the value each type of metadata provides helps to prioritize iterations of building the entire solution.

Industry experts recognize several metadata architecture approaches and variations within those approaches. These options are reviewed below.

4.8.1. *Architecture scenario 1: point-to-point metadata architecture*

The point-to-point metadata architecture has an independent metadata repository for each tool (software application) that creates metadata. For example, a data modeling tool creates and maintains this business metadata (logical data model, entity/attribute name, definition, etc.) and is also the metadata repository tool that will be accessed and updated for that type of metadata. Similarly, BI applications contain metadata about reports, calculations and data derivations and consumers of data, and data integration software contains metadata on lineage.

The sharing of metadata occurs directly between the applications. There is no single integration point. This type of metadata architecture is simpler to implement, but it is not the ideal solution because of the difficulty involved in integrating the metadata.

Point-to-point strengths:

– simplest to implement, good starting point

Point-to-point weaknesses:

– short-term solution because of the difficulty involved in integrating metadata, to support complex searches and consolidate metadata views;

– limited support for resolving semantic differences across tools;

– need to build highly customized metadata presentation layers by user type;

– does not support automated impact analysis.

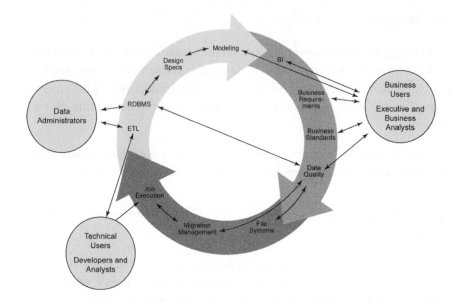

Figure 4.2. *Scenario 1: point-to-point metadata architecture. For a color version of this figure, see www.iste.co.uk/laurent/data.zip*

4.8.2. *Architecture scenario 2: hub and spoke metadata architecture*

The hub and spoke metadata architecture consists of a centralized repository that stores all metadata from each tool that creates metadata. The central repository is the hub, and the spokes are applications such as data modeling tool, BI applications and data integration software. The hub and spoke metadata architecture represents the ideal state for metadata management, but is rarely attained because of cost and complexity of implementation.

It is not uncommon for large-scale, robust implementations to require several years of effort and substantial cost to the organization. In the end, the complexity and expense that arise from building a presentation layer for business users, delivering an integrated view of metadata and addressing granularity and semantic differences between business and technical metadata often prevent centralized architectures from achieving the desired return on investment.

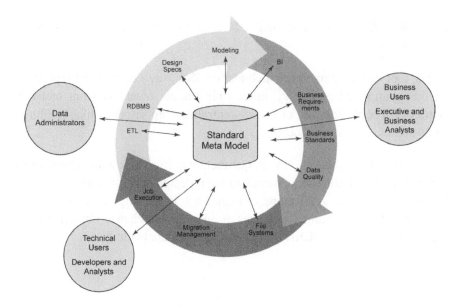

Figure 4.3. *Scenario 2: hub and spoke metadata architecture. For a color version of this figure, see www.iste.co.uk/laurent/data.zip*

Hub and spoke strengths:

– ideal state for metadata management;

– supports highly customized metadata presentation layers by user type;

– enables advanced searches;

– supports automated impact analysis across tools.

Hub and spoke weaknesses:

– rarely attained because of cost and complexity of implementation;

– relies on a repository tool with extensive metadata exchange bridges;

– requires extensive customization, requiring several years of effort and cost;

– usually does not achieve the desired return on investment.

4.8.3. *Architecture scenario 3: tool of record metadata architecture*

The tool of record metadata architecture also uses a centralized repository, but this centralized repository stores only unique metadata from metadata sources of record. The tool of record centralized repository is like building a data warehouse for metadata.

For example, it collects only unique metadata from a data modeling source of record and will not collect metadata from design specification documents. The tool of record architecture is somewhat less complex to implement; however, it faces the same challenges as any data warehouse implementation (e.g. semantic and granularity issues during metadata loading).

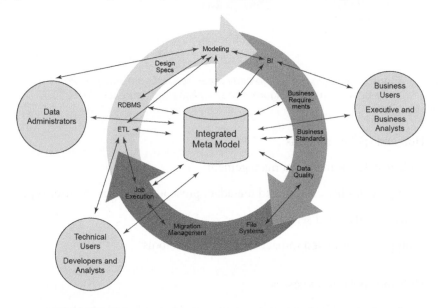

Figure 4.4. *Scenario 3: tool of record metadata architecture. For a color version of this figure, see www.iste.co.uk/laurent/data.zip*

Tool of record strengths:

– supports highly customized metadata presentation layers by user type;

– enables advanced searches;

– supports automated impact analysis across tools;

– less complex to implement than hub and spoke because it only collects unique metadata, not all.

Tool of record weaknesses:

– relies on customization;

– faces same challenges of any data warehouse implementation (e.g. semantic and granularity issue resolution before metadata loading).

4.8.4. *Architecture scenario 4: hybrid metadata architecture*

The hybrid metadata architecture uses some of the architectural highlights from the other architectures. A few tools are selected as metadata repositories or registries. Point-to-point interfaces are created from metadata sources to these repositories. The hybrid metadata architecture removes some complexity and expense involved in implementing a centralized repository. It leverages the enterprise tools that are already being used for design, development and maintenance of data and metadata.

Hybrid strengths:

– limits the number of repository-to-repository interfaces, therefore removing some of the complexity and expense of found in other solutions;

– supports highly customized presentation layers, advanced searches and partial automation of impact analysis across tools;

– easier implementation and maintenance;

– leverages an organization's current tools and expands on them, lowering initial investment;

– allows migration to a centralized repository to occur in steps.

Hybrid weaknesses:

– metadata answers are not all in a single location.

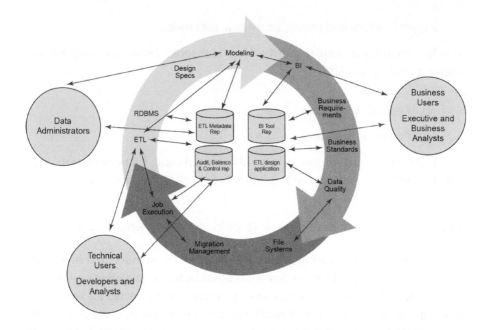

Figure 4.5. *Scenario 4: hybrid metadata architecture. For a color version of this figure, see www.iste.co.uk/laurent/data.zip*

4.8.5. *Architecture scenario 5: federated metadata architecture*

The federated metadata architecture described below will further expand on the hybrid metadata architecture with a more current look at what is being considered today. The federated repository can be considered a *virtual enterprise metadata repository*. An architecture for the federated repository would look something like Figure 4.6.

We see at the bottom of the diagram a series of separate sources of metadata and other metadata repositories, some located on *premise* and some located in the cloud (public or private). Virtualization is achieved through a series of connectors, with each connector designed to access the metadata held within the source system or repository. These connectors provide a means of abstraction to the integrated metadata store. This system comprises of automated services to ingest new metadata or analyze new data stores as they are added to the overall integrated metadata system. Finally, a single-user experience allows both business and IT users to find, access and view metadata. The portal provides different search methods such as SQL, free text and graph, in order to allow different communities to search for the metadata they are most interested in. The portal also provides collaboration to allow users to tag or provide additional descriptions and commentary on the metadata.

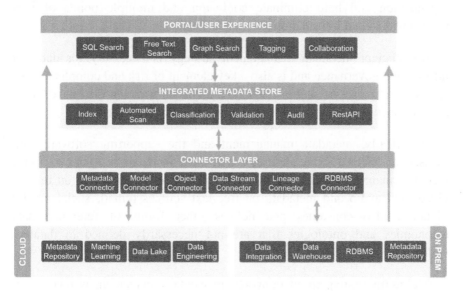

Figure 4.6. *Scenario 5: federated metadata architecture. For a color version of this figure, see www.iste.co.uk/laurent/data.zip*

Federated strengths are the following:

– focused on automated curation and providing a single view of metadata to the user;

– easier implementation and maintenance;

– leverages an organization's current tools and expands on them, lowering initial investment.

Federated weaknesses are the following:

– not ideally suited for manual metadata curation;

– limited market toolset to provide the virtualization;

– architectural approach and software still maturing.

4.9. Metadata management

Readily available metadata allows business users to easily find, use and analyze data. They provide a foundation for consistent data use throughout an organization and help eliminate confusion and multiple points of view regarding data and information.

An efficient metadata management strategy is necessary for data and information governance and is also a key element of risk and compliance as it can address questions such as: What data and information do I have? What types of documents do I have? Where they are? Are they secure?

Historically, metadata management and the supporting software were focused on metadata that describes data held in database systems. Today, metadata management extends to document metadata, metadata on images, video, and audio and metadata on free-text sources (email, social media). Metadata also consumes and defines other forms of reference data, taxonomies and ontologies that are not necessarily defined in database systems.

Metadata management context: metadata management is involved in many other information management areas. Figure 4.7 illustrates how metadata management relates to other systems and initiatives within information management and examples of what metadata is exchanged between them.

The left-hand side of the figure depicts primarily metadata producers. The metadata produced is consumed and managed by the metadata management system which then distributes relevant metadata to downstream systems, shown mainly on the right-hand side. There are some systems that are both producers and consumers of metadata.

The systems in Figure 4.7 are described below with details of the type of metadata exchanged.

Metadata management: the metadata management component is responsible for consuming, managing, distributing and publishing all forms of metadata. Metadata is consumed in various ways: ingestion, direct read, scraping or use of machine learning or other cognitive technologies. Management is concerned with lifecycle management, data definitions and matching data items. Metadata is then distributed to or published for (API) downstream systems. The metadata management component also includes the metadata catalog, which is a business-facing interface that allows business users search, discover and understand data.

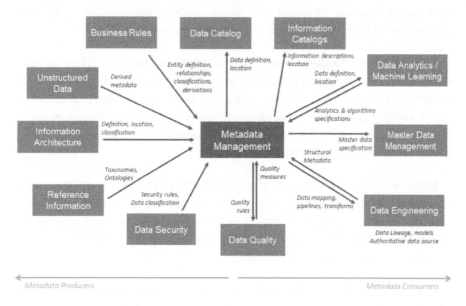

Figure 4.7. *Metadata management system context*

Business rules: business rules should be considered as the starting point for information management. A business rule will provide the high-level definition of an entity, which is then detailed further within the metadata management system. Business rules also define relations between data and how data is used by business processes, specifying where data is created and consumed. If an organization defines business rules in an application, then this information can be consumed to a metadata management system.

Unstructured data: metadata is also extracted from unstructured data sources, for example, a library of images can be analyzed and then metadata identified for those images, which includes information about the image content as well as basic details such as image size, the owner and date created. Automation can be used to derive image content metadata.

Information architecture: the structural design, storage, organization, lifecycle management and sharing of information fall under information architecture. It is similar in scope to enterprise information management. In this context, information architecture provides metadata on documents including descriptive metadata (file name, author, version, date), location information and classification and category information.

Reference information: ontologies, taxonomies and other reference data also feed into the metadata management system where they provide standard definitions for classification and categorization. An ontology provides a formal naming and definition of data within a domain. A taxonomy provides the hierarchical classification of entities of interest to an organization. It also defines the rules by which entities are classified.

Data security: the data security component is typically part of a wider information security initiative. A key piece of metadata produced by the data security component is the security classification of data, whether it is public, confidential, or private. It may also define the availability of the data, who is allowed access to different sets of data.

Data quality: data quality both shares and consumes metadata. Business rules define the quality standard for a piece of data, and this is shared to data quality via the metadata management system. In practice, however, data quality rules tend to be defined directly in the data quality tool as part of a data quality exercise implemented to improve data quality. Data quality systems, if implemented, measure the quality of data against the defined rule. The results of the analysis are ingested by the metadata management tool. The data quality results are then shared with data engineering and with reporting and analytical tools.

Data engineering: data engineering is concerned with the structure of data, how it is stored and how it relates to other data. It also defines interfaces between systems of record and building processes that move data between these systems and ingestion of data into data analytical platforms; it therefore also defines the authoritative sources of data. Therefore, data engineering consumes large amounts of metadata; data engineers need to understand source data structures and relationships between data and data quality results to manage bad data and data security considerations. Formal data modeling tools are used here, and the metadata created by these tools is ingested by the metadata management system.

Master data management: from business rules and data architecture, the metadata management system defines which data is considered master data and what source is considered the authoritative data source, and this information is consumed by master data management systems.

Data analytics, machine learning: the data analytics, machine learning item is primarily a consumer of metadata as well as creating metadata. Data analytics, which here includes reporting, dashboards, visualization, self-service, data analysis and statistical analysis, uses the metadata catalog to identify and understand the source data.

The reports, dashboards and analytics that are created are then sources of metadata themselves and become sources of information that propagate back to the information catalogs.

In a similar manner, machine learning also consumes metadata to identify and understand the data used for the machine learning algorithms. The algorithms and the predictions or other results from the machine learning process are themselves sources of metadata and are so consumed by metadata management. For example, machine learning can be used to extract structured data from raw text or analyze images to identify subjects within the image or to classify documents. The machine learning in these cases is typically executed by the operational system; however, the resulting metadata should be managed and propagated through the metadata management system.

Data derivations: how data is manipulated, calculated or aggregated should be defined by business rules and then consumed via metadata by analytical tools, although in reality, this is rarely the case.

Information catalogs: an information catalog provides a means to identify and locate a wide variety of information. Like a data catalog (described below), a businessperson would use the information catalog to search for information and the catalog would then provide locations or links to that information. The information catalog may contain an index of information held within documents, but is not responsible for the information itself.

Data catalogs: data catalogs are a large consumer of metadata, primarily data definitions, descriptions and sources of data. The relation between metadata management and data catalogs is described in more detail in the next section.

Note that there are other relations between these components which, for clarity, are not depicted in the diagram. For example, the data security component defines the integrity requirement for a data item and this is shared with the data quality component, which is responsible for ensuring compliance to the integrity requirement.

4.10. Metadata and data lakes

Metadata is crucial in any ecosystem based on a data lake. Indeed, when dealing with huge reservoirs of raw data, the following questions must be answered clearly:

– Where do the data come from?

– Are the data reliable?

– Who may use the data?

– Which transformations have been done on the data?

– What is the structure of the data?

In a data lake ecosystem, as well as other information systems, metadata are varied and pervasive [RIL 17]. Moreover, metadata are produced and used at all interoperability levels in order to provide a description of data sources, with the goal of easing data querying and information retrieval.

In order to meet all needs regarding metadata in an ecosystem based on a data lake, we propose a model including metadata. To do so, our model consists of three abstract independent but complementary layers referred to as *applications and workloads*, *data* and *systems* (see Figure 4.8). Thus, in our model, each layer encapsulates a specific kind of metadata.

4.10.1. *Application and workload layer*

4.10.1.1. *Workload metadata*

The workload is a description of the processing streams applied to the data in a given period of time. In our model, this description is seen as a metadata source and is computed based on the source code of the processes, the files storing these processes and the associated logs [HAL 16a]. Examples of workload metadata are the following:

– information on data lineage and provenance [HAL 16a, TEA 18b, HAI 16];

– statistics or an index for query optimization regarding running processes. Querying the runtime engine about the state of running processes is useful, in particular for system recovery in case of failure, or for near-time integration [FER 15]);

– statistics on runtime performance, needed for optimization [HAI 16].

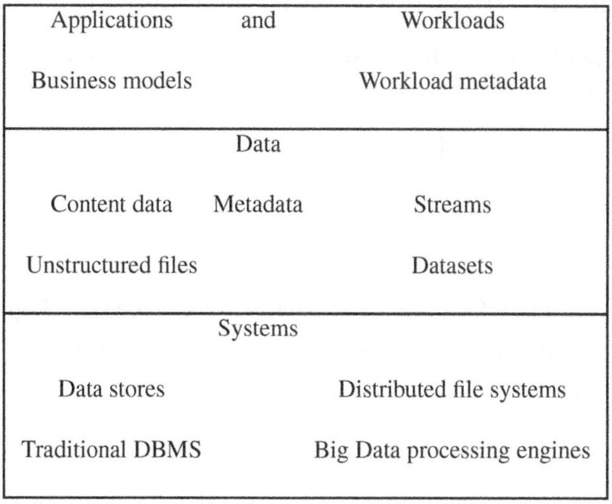

Applications	and	Workloads
Business models		Workload metadata
	Data	
Content data	Metadata	Streams
Unstructured files		Datasets
	Systems	
Data stores		Distributed file systems
Traditional DBMS		Big Data processing engines

Figure 4.8. *Metadata layers in an ecosystem based on a data lake*

4.10.1.2. *Business models*

Metadata related to a business model provide a context to data used in a specific application or workload. Such metadata consist of annotations defined by an expert, specific rules or policies for monitoring the application, crowdsourcing knowledge [HAL 16a], rules related to data quality [CHU 13, DAL 13], statistical models and definitions of metrics for assessing the data processes of the data lake [HAI 16, DAL 13]. Examples of such metadata follow:

– an enterprise glossary, i.e. a catalog of objects and concepts specific to the considered domain of the ecosystem [TEA 18b, MAI 17, THE 17];

– integrity constraints related to the domain, such as official regulations or physical constraints necessary for managing and optimizing data streams produced by sensors [FIS 10];

– business rules that have an impact on data cleaning, curating or repairing [DAL 13, STO 13];

– governance policies: security, access control, compliance, quality assurance, legitimacy [HAL 16a, TEA 18b, TER 15];

– standardization through creating new data or metadata types defined by a data steward [TEA 18b];

– probabilistic models [DAL 13].

4.10.2. *Data layer*

In this layer, metadata are defined from the content, datasets and data streams, along with their associated metadata. These sources are explained below.

4.10.2.1. *Content*

Data contained in a data lake are heterogeneous, coming from flat files, from databases of any kind (relational, NoSQL, etc.) or from data streams [FIS 10].

The metadata generated from the content are:

1) statistics to be used in profiling services or in interfaces for monitoring the content of the ecosystem;

2) data schema, needed for an effective data retrieval in the ecosystem;

3) inferred or aggregated information ([HAI 16, HAL 16a]), such as new discovered schemas, schema abstracts, new discovered relations and new classes for logically grouping data;

4) rules implementing integrity constraints or validity rules for query optimization and consistency preservation;

5) an index to speed up or ease the access to important data. Indexes may also provide generic information on the storage (e.g. the medium or the file) in the ecosystem.

To get metadata from the content, extraction operations, analysis or machine learning techniques can be used.

4.10.2.2. Data streams

Data streams coming from connected objects such as sensors or smart meters contain dynamic metadata (such as the time the data were generated) as well as static metadata (such as the schema of the data or integrity constraints, holding for long enough to be considered as static).

4.10.2.3. Datasets

Datasets consist of data files to be stored in the data lake for the purpose of experimentations. These data can be structured, semi-structured or unstructured, and their associated metadata are data schema, descriptive metadata [HAL 16a] or annotations [TEA 18a].

As an example of descriptive metadata for smart grid data (as extracted from the Open Data platform):

– licence: open licence;

– availability: from 2012/07/26 to 2013/08/08;

– frequency: occasional;

– creation: 2015/05/11;

– modification: 2016/01/11.

4.10.2.4. Metadata

Metadata are themselves data on which processes are run to produce other metadata. These produced metadata are, for example, schema abstracts, recommendations for data processing (e.g. join computation [HAI 16]) or the description of data distribution in datasets.

4.10.3. *System layer*

This layer deals with storage media (such as distributed file systems) and data processing systems (e.g. relational DBMS, NoSQL systems, analytics engines). Metadata of this layer are used for monitoring, scheduling and optimizing the engines of a data lake system. These metadata are the following:

– timestamps, used for data stream processing [FIS 10], near-time data integration [FER 15], or for providing information on the runtime progression;

– metadata files corresponding to physical data storage [HAL 16a];

– metrics and statistics on the usage of the different storage systems of the ecosystem. These data allow us to automatically balance data distribution among the storage systems.

4.10.4. *Metadata types*

Metadata types in data lakes are designed based on generic types set by international consortiums such as NISO [RIL 17]. The classification of these types may, however, differ from one consortium to the other.

In order to better characterize the semantics of metadata in a data lake ecosystem, metadata can be classified according to their creation mode and their role in the management of the information system. User-generated metadata are distinguished from system-generated metadata so as to ensure that metadata are expressive enough to fully account for all abstraction levels needed by humans on the one hand and by machines on the other hand.

Another possible metadata classification can be done according to the processing needed to generate them. In this case, two categories are considered: explicit metadata and implicit metadata. In the former case, metadata can be obtained either directly or through light processes (such metadata are those stored along with the data). In the latter case, metadata are obtained through more involved processes such as content analysis, statistic computation or logical inference.

Another possible classification can be defined based on the lifetime of metadata, considering that static metadata are stored in the system, whereas dynamic metadata are stored in a cache (in particular when dealing with data streams).

Other types of metadata have been proposed in the literature related to ecosystems based on data lakes. These types are listed below.

4.10.4.1. *Operational metadata*

According to NISO classification, operational metadata describe data in the system and are used for an efficient management of operations on data. These metadata consist of indexes, timestamps and information encoded in a data source when integrated.

For example, in the case of goods datasets [HAL 16a], these metadata are: the path leading to the data files, the size of the dataset, the access date and the name of the dataset owner.

4.10.4.2. *Structural or schema metadata*

These metadata provide a description of the structure of the data objects [WIK 18, ABD 16] and should be distinguished from the data schema that concerns the actual organization of the data according to three levels, as recalled below:

– physical level: a description of the files where the data are stored and of the associated indexes;

– conceptual level: an abstract description of the way data are modeled in the system to be used (in relational DBMS, this description is based on the notion of a table);

– business level: a refinement of the conceptual level based on specific access controls, transformation operations, or constraints for security enforcement.

In this context, structural metadata are used for the design of data architecture, of consistency maintenance protocols and of query and process optimization [FIS 10].

4.10.4.3. *Semantic metadata*

As mentioned in [HAL 16a, TEA 18b], these metadata are meant to provide a context to the data so as experts of the application domain, who are not experts in data science, can nevertheless exploit their data. Basically, these metadata allow for categorizing, annotating or tagging the data.

For example, consider the case of a data lake in which, among other kinds of data, tweets are stored and annotated. If, as in [HAI 16], a statistician wishes to analyze datasets containing tweets, and this user is not an expert in query languages and does not know where exactly the relevant data are stored, then a simple global query mentioning the key word "twitter" can allow for the retrieval of relevant data.

A specific case of semantic metadata is that of annotations using "collaborative" tags. These tags correspond to conventional agreements by the data producers and thus allow for setting basic rules to standardize names, so as members of a given department or project can easily identify their own data. Citing, again, [HAI 16], such tags improve the communication between members of a given group, while allowing for access controls between users from different groups.

4.10.4.4. *Lineage metadata*

These metadata are used in data governance [TEA 18b] for tracking the provenance and the use of the data throughout the ecosystem. These metadata are composed of references to versions corresponding to the processing and to transformations operated on the data.

4.10.4.5. *User-defined metadata*

These metadata are issued by experts of the considered domain [TEA 18b] or by a user wishing to identify useful data. Such metadata are metrics of probability models, business rules or meta models and predefined types.

4.10.4.6. *Inferred metadata*

These metadata are generated by the system, through specific algorithms such as clustering, inference or statistics.

Examples of such metadata are similarity and duplication search [HAL 16a], schema discovery, inconsistency detection or alerts [HAI 16].

4.11. Metadata management in data lakes

As earlier mentioned, metadata are data and thus, metadata in data lakes have to be properly managed. In this section, we address this issue by giving hints on how to organize their storage, how to store them, how to discover them, how to define their lineage, how to query them and how to select the related data sources.

4.11.1. *Metadata directory*

The metadata directory gathers all metadata in a knowledge base [HAI 16, HAL 16a, TEA 18b] whose structure is defined by a "metadata schema". In the knowledge base, metadata are organized according to a catalog (see section 4.2.2).

This metadata catalog is built up by experts of the application domain, independently from the processes for data processing. The goal of this catalog is to provide the necessary knowledge to properly monitor all services offered by the data ecosystem. This catalog can thus be seen as a reference dictionary for the identification and control of the data stored in the data lake. Consequently, the catalog allows for the alignment of the data management strategy and the business model of the enterprise. We note that the catalog may also contain the definition of new types for structuring the metadata that are to be extracted from and stored in the system. The management of these metadata is ensured by specific modules, such as the type system in Atlas [TEA 18b].

On the other hand, the component managing the metadata repertory contains basic features for inserting, updating and accessing metadata, whereas further advanced features may be available (e.g. model management). All these features are referred to in other components, either internal to the component in charge of managing metadata (such as features for metadata search or for metadata extraction), or external to this component (such as components for the management of auditing metadata, security, access policies and regulation systems).

4.11.2. *Metadata storage*

In a data lake ecosystem, the storage of the data and their associated metadata is done during the initial loading phase, as well as during every updating phase of the ecosystem. The process of storage of the metadata is launched upon the following events:

– the extraction of metadata encoded in data objects or metadata deduced through some content analysis [HAI 16, HAL 16a, HAL 16a, QUI 16];

– the classification of metadata done by experts of the domain, as discussed in the previous section [HAI 16, HAL 16a, QUI 16, TEA 18b].

4.11.3. *Metadata discovery*

The metadata discovery process runs as a background process of many other processes, with the goal of detecting implicit metadata that have not been extracted during the initial loading phase.

These metadata can be constraints, such as keys found through data analysis, provenance relationships found in the data lineage or content similarities. The discovery of metadata is achieved through mappings or inference as described below:

1) mappings between metadata. Such a mapping is useful when, for example, two distinct names are given to similar objects, and more generally for taking into account synonymy between terms. These mappings are based on content similarities defining clusters or on explicit links (such as "has_a" or "is_of" links) between data and metadata expressed through ontologies;

2) inferences lead on metadata allow for the extraction of relevant new knowledge or recommendations. We also recall that inferring metadata can be achieved based on content analysis [HAL 16a].

4.11.4. *Metadata lineage*

Lineage processing allows us to collect information on the evolution of datasets so as to make the ecosystem reliable [HAI 16, HAL 16a, HAL 16a, TEA 18b]. More precisely, lineage on data describes the transformations, the different states, the characteristics and the quality of these data during the processing chain.

Roughly, when a set A is transformed into a set B by a process P, the transformed data B are stored in the data lake, and the corresponding service creates, in the metadata directory, a triple containing references to sets A and B and to the process P. The construction of the lineage works according to the following two different modes:

– ad hoc mode, whereby the lineage elements are built up progressively when processes are run. This mode yields an important overhead when many processes are run or when metadata are managed in a centralized environment;

– post hoc mode, whereby the lineage elements are built up after the execution of the processes, based on the logs of these processes. This mode is more suitable to scale up with large volumes of data, but might entail data consistency issues.

4.11.5. *Metadata querying*

When querying metadata, the expected answer is the set of data associated in the data lake to the metadata specified by the query. These queries are generally complex queries expressed in various languages, based either on natural language or on SQL (such as DSL in ATLAS [TEA 18b]). Examples of such queries, expressed in natural language are: (i) give the data produced by job J or (ii) give the version number of those data whose processing has been allowed to user U.

This metadata querying component is used in many services, among which we cite ([HAI 16, HAL 16a, TEA 18b]):

– content profiling;

– advanced search features;

– dashboards for monitoring the data lake;

– auditing features and quality assessment.

4.11.6. *Data source selection*

The choice of whether a new data source should be integrated relies on information such as the estimated cost of data importation or the estimated coverage of values by the dataset [TER 15] and quality of the data.

Further information are also considered, such as, for example, the license for exploiting the data (the producer may impose that the processes on open data be open), or the way the source is accessed (e.g. importing data in batch mode may have an impact on the performance of the source [PAS 15]).

Moreover, many sources may have similar content, in which case choosing one rather than another must be suggested through metadata, informing on the cost of loading, the storage size or specific regulations set by the data owner.

4.12. Metadata and master data management

Master data management (MDM) is the effort made by an organization to create one single master reference source for critical business data. As it can be expensive, not all data are mastered, but only those that will give the greatest benefit, typically this means mastering customer data to provide a single view of a customer. This book includes a dedicated MDM chapter to deep-dive into the concept and its link with the data lake.

MDM solutions comprise a broad range of data cleansing, transformation and integration practices. As data sources are added to the system, MDM initiates processes to identify, collect, transform and repair data. Some solutions also provide automatic inference of master data through scanning and analyzing data sources. Once the data meet the quality thresholds, schemas and taxonomies are created to help maintain a high-quality master reference.

Metadata is used to support MDM initiatives and solutions as metadata can define the source, type, description and quality of data that needs to be mastered.

4.13. Conclusion

Heterogeneous data ecosystems today rely on data lake systems. Those systems favor the schema-on-read approach for data ingestion [ERL 16]. Ingestion without data integration may, over time, cause data silos to appear in the lake. Data transformation and integration can be done in a later phase with an effective management of metadata. This chapter first provided (i) two different classifications of metadata identified from existing systems [HAI 16, TEA 18b, TEA 18a, FIS 10, TER 15, STO 13, HAL 16a, QUI 16] and then (ii) introduced the different services for metadata management and processing that are relevant in data lake ecosystems.

5

A Use Case of Data Lake Metadata Management

To govern a data lake with a great volume of heterogeneous types of data, metadata management is mandatory to prevent the data lake from being turned into a data swamp which is invisible, incomprehensible and inaccessible to users. In this chapter, we present a use case of data lake metadata management, applied to the health-care field, which is particularly known by its heterogeneous sources of data.

We first present a more detailed data lake definition in comparison to the chapter dedicated to the data lake definition and its underlying data lake architecture, based on which we designed the metadata model. Second, we present a metadata classification pointing to the essential attributes adapted to the use case. Third, we introduce a conceptual model of metadata which considers different types: (i) structured, (ii) semi-structured and (iii) unstructured raw or processed data. Fourth, we validate our proposition with an implementation of the conceptual model which concerns two DBMSs (one relational database and one NoSQL database).

5.1. Context

The University Hospital Center (UHC) of Toulouse is the largest hospital center in the south of France. Approximately 4,000 doctors and 12,000

Chapter written by Imen MEGDICHE, Franck RAVAT and Yan ZHAO.

hospital staff ensure more than 280,000 stays and 850,000 consultations per year. The information system of the hospital stores all the patient data including medical images, biological results, textual hospital reports, PMSI (Programme de médicalisation des systèmes d'information) [CHA 17] administrative information related as well as administration data, to the functioning of the hospital. With the aim of improving medical treatment and optimizing the patient pathways, Toulouse UHC investigates a data lake project. The objective of the project is to ingest all the heterogeneous structural types of internal data and some external medical data that the UHC can access in order to provide a global view and foster new perspectives for data analytics by different users (data scientists, data analysts and BI professionals). The project respects an incrementally iterative process. The first iteration concerns ingesting two datasets in the data lake and processing the data to establish two data marts.

To govern the data lake, which can contain heterogeneous and voluminous data, we have designed a metadata management system for the data lake and implemented two proofs of concept in order to validate the system. With the aim of presenting the metadata management system adapted to the project, we first propose a definition of data lake and a data lake functional architecture, based on which we designed the metadata management.

5.1.1. *Data lake definition*

As mentioned in the previous chapter dedicated to the data lake definition, the data lake concept is initially put forward in the industrial world. It was then defined in both academic and industrial worlds [CAM 15, FAN 15, HAI 16, LLA 18, MAD 16, MIL 16, DUL 15, WAL 15, RAV 19a]. All the existing definitions respect the idea that a data lake stores raw data in their native format. However, different definitions emphasize different aspects of data lakes (see Figure 5.1). Regarding input, the author of [FAN 15] presents that the input of a data lake is the internal data of an organization. Regarding process, the author of [MIL 16] introduces that there is no data process during the ingestion phase and [CAM 15, HAI 16, MIL 16, DUL 15] introduce that data will be processed upon usage. Regarding architecture, [FAN 15] presents that data lakes are based on an architecture with low-cost technologies. Regarding governance, metadata management is emphasized in

[HAI 16, WAL 15]. And regarding users, [MAD 16] presents that data scientists and statisticians are data lake users.

	Reference	Input	Ingestion	Storage	Process	Output	Governance	Architecture	Users
Academic definition	[FAN 15]	Data within an enterprise		Large quantity of raw data				Low cost technologies	
	[ALR 15]			Data in their raw format			Meta-data	Flat functional architecture	
	[MIL 13]		No process	A vast amount of raw data in their native format		Raw data until they are needed and used			
	[HAI 16]			Raw data		Raw on-demand integration	Meta-data		
	[MAD 16]			Data in their raw format			Meta-data Data governance		Data scientist Data statistician
	[LLA 18]			Large quantity and variety of data	Data process				
Industrial	[CAM 15] [DUL 15]			Large amount of raw data in native format		Raw data when they are needed			

Figure 5.1. *Data lake definitions*

Existing definitions have evolved over time from experience feedback. Nevertheless, as mentioned, these different definitions are vague, they are not integrated with each other or even contradictory. To be as complete as possible and to answer the requirements of Toulouse UHC, we propose a definition that includes input, process, output and governance of data lakes:

A data lake is a Big Data analytics solution that ingests heterogeneously structured raw data from various sources (local or external to the organization) and stores these raw data in their native format, allows us to process data according to different requirements and provides access of available data to different users (data scientists, data analysts, BI professionals, etc.) for statistical analysis, Business Intelligence (BI), Machine Learning (ML), etc., and governs data to ensure the data quality, data security and data lifecycle.

5.1.2. *Data lake functional architecture*

After proposing a data lake definition adapted to the project, the next point that we study is a functional architecture of a data lake. To the best of our knowledge, a recognised data lake architecture does not exist in the literature. Data lake functional architecture has evolved from mono-zone to multi-zone, and it is always presented with technical solutions (see Figure 5.2).

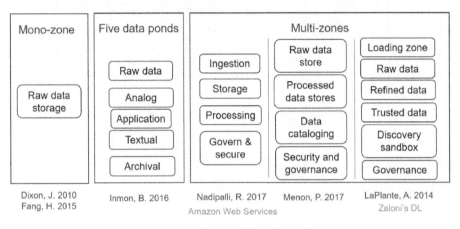

Figure 5.2. *Data lake functional architecture evolution*

The first vision [FAN 15, DIX 10] of the data lake architecture was a flat architecture with mono-zone that is closely tied to the HADOOP environment. This zone allows the collection and storage raw data in their native formats. It includes the data from web logs, sensor devices, operational data store (ODS) and online transaction processing (OLTP) systems. The advantage of this architecture is to enable the loading of heterogeneous and voluminous data at low cost. However, this architecture is simple and can hardly be realized, especially in the context of Big Data analytics. As a matter of fact, this architecture does not reflect the activities performed by users, such as the pre-processing phases inherent in decision analyses with a set of intermediate data storage.

A second vision of data lake architecture contains five data ponds [MAD 16]. A raw data pond that stores the just ingested data and the data that do not fit in other ponds. The analog, application and textual data ponds store classified data from, raw data pond the by their characteristics. An archival data pond stores the data that are no longer used. This architecture classifies different types of data and discards useless data, which makes data finding faster and data analytics easier. However, the division of different ponds – the archival pond, in particular, cannot ensure the availability of all the raw data – contradicts the general recognition of data lake which is to ingest all the raw data and process them upon usage.

To overcome these drawbacks, a third vision of architecture with multi-zones is proposed with a more diverse technological environment in the academic and industrial worlds. The author of [NAD 17] presents Amazon Web Services (AWS) data lake architecture with four zones: ingestion, storage, processing, and govern and secure. Raw data are loaded in the ingestion zone. The ingested raw data are stored in the storage zone. When data are needed, they are processed in the processing zone. The objective of the govern and secure zone is to control data security, data quality, metadata management and data lifecycle. The author of [MEN 17] separates the data processing zone into batch-processing and real-time processing zones. He also adds a processed data zone to store all the cleansed data. Zaloni's data lake architecture [LAP 14] separates the processing and storage zones into refined data zone, trusted data zone and discovery sandbox zone. The refined zone allows us to integrate and structure data. The trusted data zone stores all the cleansed data. Data for exploratory analysis moves to the discovery sandbox.

As mentioned, a lot of data lake architectures are supported with technical solutions. They are not independent of the inherent technical environment. Consequently, none of the existing architectures draw a clear distinction between functionality-related and technology-related components. What is more, the concept of multi-zone architecture is interesting and deserves further investigation. We believe that some zones are essential, while others are optional or can be regrouped. Concerning the essential zones, based on our data lake definition, a data lake should be able to ingest raw data, process data upon usage, store processed data, provide access for different uses and govern data.

Unlike several proposals, we need to distinguish functional architecture from technical architecture; this is because a functional architecture concerns the usage perspective and it can be implemented by different technical solutions. By adopting the existing data lake architectures and avoiding their shortcomings, we propose a functional data lake architecture (see Figure 5.3), which contains four essential zones, with each having a treatment area (dotted rectangle) and a data storage area that stores the result of processes (gray rectangle):

– *raw data zone*: all types of data are ingested without processing and are stored in their native format. The ingestion can be batch, real-time or hybrid. This zone allows users to find the original version of data for their analysis to facilitate subsequent treatments;

– *process zone*: in this zone, users can transform data according to their requirements and store all the intermediate transformations. The data processing includes batch and/or real-time processing. This zone allows users to process data (selection, projection, join, aggregation, normalization etc.) for their data analysis;

– *access zone*: users can put all the prepared data in the access zone which stores all the available data and provides data access. This zone allows users to access data for self-service data consumption for different analytics (reporting, statistical analysis, business intelligence analysis, machine learning algorithms);

– *governance zone*: data governance is applied on all the other zones. It is in charge of ensuring data security, data quality, data lifecycle, data access and metadata management.

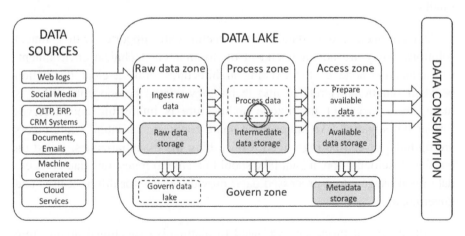

Figure 5.3. *Data lake functional architecture*

To exemplify our architecture, we propose an implementation as depicted in Figure 5.4. Raw datasets (RD1, RD2) are ingested in the data lake and stored in the raw data zone in their native format. Data are processed in the process zone and all the intermediate datasets (PD1, PD2, PD3, PD4) are stored in this area too. All the available data (AD1, AD2, AD3) are stored in the access zone for data consumption.

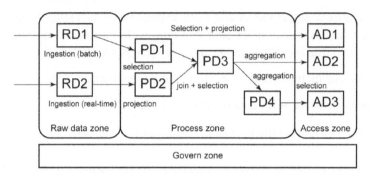

Figure 5.4. *An implementation of the data lake functional architecture*

As we can see in the example of data lake functional architecture, the ingestion zone stores different types of datasets, the process zone can process different datasets in many steps and the access zone can ensure the availability of raw datasets, as well as processed datasets. Therefore, a metadata management is important to govern all the datasets in a data lake.

5.2. Related work

Given that the data lake is a relatively new concept, there is not much scientific work on metadata management for data lakes. In this section, we present an overview of related work on this field by largely referring to articles in subject fields like data warehouses and Big Data. Note that we will use *dataset* concept, in this chapter: *a dataset is a collection of data which can be a relational database, a spreadsheet, a textual document, a log file or another type of file.*

5.2.1. *Metadata classification*

Regarding data warehouses, there are mainly two classifications of metadata. [PON 04] classified metadata by technical, operational and business. [GAB 10, FOS 07] classified metadata by definitional, data quality, navigational and data lineage.

Metadata classifications of Big Data, especially of data lakes were inspired by these two classifications of data warehouses. In the context of data lakes, a first classification identifies three categories [ORA 15, LOP 14]:

– *technical* includes data type, format and the structure (schema);

– *operational* includes data processing information;

– *business* includes the business names and descriptions.

However, we think business metadata are not necessary for data lakes because:

– different types of data from different sources are ingested and stored in a data lake without predefined needs;

– when data scientists try to dig out potential value of data, they may not have business aims.

What is more, the first classification consists of information about each dataset, it does not include relationships between different datasets. However, the relationships are important to help users find relevant datasets in data lakes.

A second classification is defined for data lakes. Metadata can be classified by inter-metadata and intra-metadata [MAC 17]. Inter-metadata describes relationships between data, it is classified by dataset containment, provenance, logical cluster and content similarity [HAL 16b]. Intra-metadata specifies each single dataset, it is classified by data characteristics, definitional, navigational, activity, lineage, rating and assessment [FOS 07, VAR 14, BIL 16, RAV 19b].

This classification concerns not only the information of each dataset but also the relationships between datasets, and both of the catalogs are classified by sub-catalogs. However, we think some sub-catalogs are not necessary for data lakes. For example, the rating category contains statistical information of user preferences, the assessment consists of dataset evaluation results such as success rate and performance of execution [VAR 14]. These two sub-catalogs are not for data lakes because datasets can be processed and analyzed by different users [CAM 15]: a dataset that makes no sense to BI professionals can be of great value to data scientists. What is more, this classification can be extended with more sub-catalogs. For example, data sensitivity and accessibility also need to be controlled in data lakes.

5.2.2. *Metadata management*

Metadata management is applied in many domains concerning data analysis, for instance, data warehouses, Big Data and data lakes.

Regarding *data warehouses*, a prototype model to ensure data security was presented in [KAT 98]. An interface of metadata by using 5W1H (what, when, who, where, why, how) was proposed in [SHI 06].

In the *Big Data* domain, with the increased volume and velocity of various types of data, the importance of metadata is underlined. [VAR 14] provided a metadata framework for next generation BI systems. [BIL 16] identified and extended the required metadata for Knowledge Discovery in Databases (KDD) and implemented a metadata repository.

In *data lakes*, metadata management is essential to enable users to search and analyze data efficiently. Different tools of metadata management implementation are introduced in [FED 17]. [NOG 18b] proposed a metadata vault model of data lakes to replace the multidimensional model. What is more, various systems of metadata management are presented. [HAL 16b] presented Google's internal data lake management system. [QUI 16] has developed a system that can automatically extract metadata from various sources and manage structural or semantic metadata by using an extensible model. [SAW 19] focused on textual documents. [ALS 16] presented a content metadata management framework to facilitate alignment. [MAC 17] proposed a system that supports data preparation in data lakes.

Although different solutions of metadata management of data lakes were proposed, authors mainly focused on a few points.

First, the detection of relationships between different datasets is always presented [HAL 16b, ALS 16, QUI 16]. Relationships between datasets can help users find the most relevant datasets possible and even check the operations or results of these datasets to facilitate data analysis. While we want to find a metadata model that shows not only the relationships between datasets but also the information of each single dataset.

Second, authors often focused on unstructured data (mostly textual data) [SAW 19, QUI 16] because it is difficult to extract information from text. However, in a data lake, there are various types of data, a model that applies to different cases is essential.

Third, data ingestion is the most considered phase to extract metadata [ALS 16, SAW 19, HAL 16b]. Nevertheless, the information produced during process and access phases has value too [FOS 07, SAW 19].

Until now, there has not been a general metadata management system that works on structured and unstructured data for the whole data lifecycle in data lakes. For our use case project, we have defined a metadata management system that addresses these weaknesses.

5.3. Metadata model

In this section, we identify a list of metadata attributes dedicated to the entire lifecycle of data in different zones of a data lake, relative to our data lake architecture. First, we propose a classification of intra- and inter-metadata. Second, we model these metadata through a conceptual model in order to implement it in a metadata management system.

5.3.1. *Metadata classification*

We propose a metadata classification by extending the second classification presented in section 2.1; this is because information on each single dataset (intra-metadata) and relationships between datasets (inter-metadata) are both important. Intra-metadata allow users to understand datasets with their characteristics, meaning, quality and security level [VAR 14, BIL 16]. Inter-metadata help users find relevant datasets that may answer their requirements to make their data discovery easier [HAL 16b, SAW 19].

– *Inter-metadata*: [HAL 16b] introduced four types of inter-metadata: dataset containment, provenance, logical cluster and content similarity. We complete the classification with partial overlap, which is not considered by other authors.

- *Dataset containment*: a dataset contains other datasets.

- *Partial overlap*: some attributes with corresponding data in some datasets overlap. For example, in a hospital, health care and billing databases contain the same attributes and data about patients, prescriptions and stays. However these two databases also contain their own data.

- *Provenance*: one dataset is produced with the data of another dataset. For example, a data mart is created with the data from a data warehouse.

- *Logical clusters*: datasets that are from the same domain. For example, different versions, duplication of the same logical dataset.

- *Content similarity*: datasets that have the same attributes.

– *Intra-metadata*:   Regarding intra-metadata, [FOS 07] proposed a data warehouse metadata classification which was extended by [VAR 14, BIL 16] in the Big Data domain. [BIL 16] classified metadata by data characteristics, definitional, navigational, activity characteristics, lineage, rating and assessment. To adapt the classification to data lakes, we retain data characteristics, definitional, navigational and lineage metadata. At the same time, we add access, quality and security metadata (see Figure 5.5).

- *Data characteristics* consist of a set of attributes that describe datasets, such as identification, name, size and creation date of datasets. This information helps users to have a general idea of a dataset. Some authors also use the word *Proprieties* to present the same thing [SAW 19].

- *Definitional metadata* specify dataset meanings. In the original taxonomy, there are vocabulary and schema subcategories. We classify definitional metadata by *semantic* and *schematic*. Structured and unstructured datasets can be described semantically with a textual description or a set of keywords (vocabularies). Schematically, structured datasets can be presented by a database schema. Definitional metadata help users understand datasets and make their data exploitation easier. In addition, users can find relevant datasets by keywords.

 - *Navigational metadata* concern the location information, for example, file paths and database connection URLs. Navigational metadata answer the question: where are the datasets that I need?

 - *Lineage metadata* present data lifecycle. It consists of the original source of datasets and the processes that have been done on the dataset. Information on dataset sources and process history makes datasets more reliable.

 - *Access metadata* present access information, for example, name of the users who accessed datasets and access tools. This information helps users to find relevant datasets by accessed users and to trust data by other users' access histories.

 - *Quality metadata* consist of data consistency and completeness [KWO 14] to ensure dataset reliability.

 - *Security metadata* consist of data sensitivity and access level. Data lakes store datasets from various sources. Some datasets may contain sensitive information that can only be accessed by certain users. Security metadata can support the verification of access. This information ensures the safety of sensitive data.

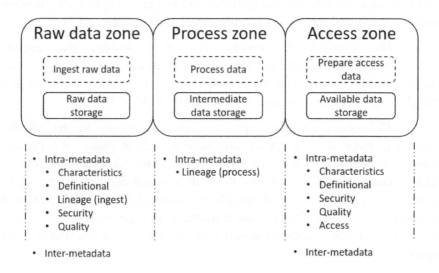

Figure 5.5. *Meta data classification*

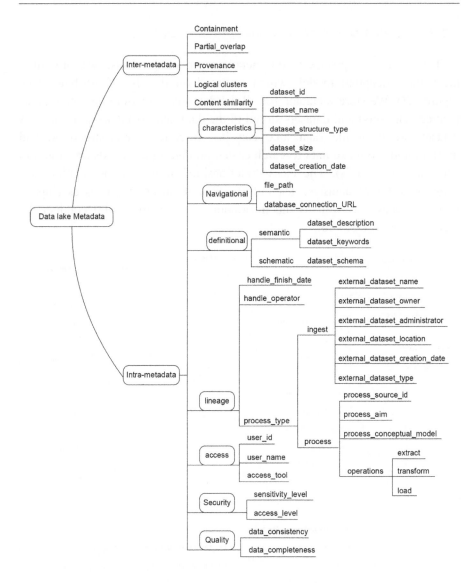

Figure 5.6. *Meta data classification*

Based on this metadata classification, we propose some essential attributes for each type of metadata (see Figure 5.6). This list of attributes is a generic and extensible modeling. Users can add or delete subcategories. The modeling can be adjusted to adopt subsequent needs.

5.3.2. *Schema of metadata conceptual model*

There are few proposals on metadata modeling. Thus, we present a metadata conceptual model, which is based on the list of attributes (see Figure 5.7). We store metadata for all the datasets, including dataset sources (source_data sets) and datasets stored in the data lake (datalake_data sets). A dataset stored in the data lake can be structured, semi-structured and unstructured. To make data research easier, all dataset keywords are stored in one class (keywords). The class "relationship" stores all the relationships between different datasets. The information of different processes (ingest, process, access) as well as the information of the users who conduct the processes are also stored.

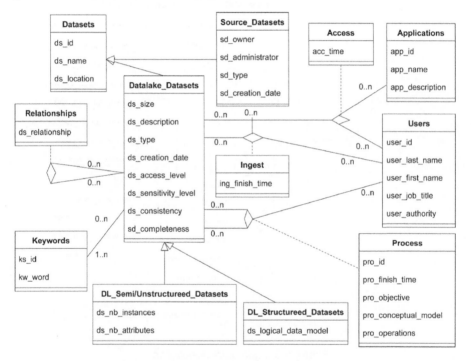

Figure 5.7. *Class diagram of metadata conceptual model*

This metadata model has several advantages:

– data sources (external datasets) are recorded;

– both structured and unstructured datasets are considered;

– all the work (ingest, process, access) that has been done in a data lake is registered;

– information of each single dataset, and relationships between different datasets are stored;

– dataset quality, sensibility and access level are controlled.

5.4. Metadata implementation

Metadata can be associated with data resources in many ways. According to [DUV 02], there are three ways to do the association: (1) embedded metadata concerns the metadata integrated into the resource by authors, for example, XML documents; (2) associated metadata is maintained in files which are tightly linked to the resources; (3) third-party metadata is maintained in an individual repository.

In data lakes, embedded metadata are not always generated in the sources because a data lake ingests and stores different types of data from various resources. It is also costly to create and manage metadata files for each dataset. For data lakes, third-party metadata is the most suitable way because an individual metadata management system can facilitate the generation and maintenance of metadata. We can consider an individual metadata system as a downstream resource; users can exploit available data thanks to its completeness. We therefore chose to implement an individual metadata management system.

When implementing such a system, different ways can be used to store metadata, as outlined in the literature. [QUI 16] uses MongoDB to store serialized JSON files. [SAW 19] presents metadata by a combination of a graph model and a data vault and stores the metadata in XML format. [ALS 16] stores metadata by ontology alignment which is based on finding similarities between datasets.

For the exploratory project of Toulouse UHC, according to the environment of the organization and the background of the project, we have first chosen to implement our solution with a relational database. This is the most used data storage in the organization. We have also chosen NoSQL to have more flexibility in the system; this way, the schema of metadata can be changed in the future to adapt the project. For the first iteration, we take five datasets (four structured and one unstructured) inside of the data lake of Toulouse UHC as an example (see Table 5.1). These five datasets are in different functional zones of the data lake (see Figure 5.8)

Dataset name	Description
ORBIS	Raw dataset of all the health care information.
SURGERY	Intermediate dataset originating from ORBIS, concerns information on surgery.
OPTIMISME_TC	Available dataset generated from SURGERY aims to optimize brain trauma procedures.
COMEDIMS	Available issued by SURGERY concerns prescriptions of expensive drugs.
COMPTE_RENDU	Raw dataset consists of scans of medical reports (pdf).

Table 5.1. *List of implemented datasets*

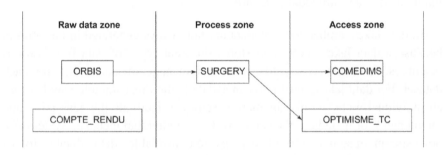

Figure 5.8. *Search datasets by keywords*

5.4.1. *Relational database*

We first implemented the conceptual model of metadata on a relational DBMS. The logical schema of RDBMS is presented in Figure 5.9 which is an implementation of the model in Figure 5.7.

With the implementation, users – for instance data analysts – can search or verify datasets according to their requirements. A user should be able to find the dataset(s) that correspond to a subject from all the datasets stored in a data lake. What is more, the system should help users to refine their analyses. Users should see all the information of the datasets that they will work on, including the information of the datasets, their source datasets and all the processes that have been done on the datasets. This is in order that users can have more confidence the data and may find some processes that can be reused to save time. To validate our proposal, we have written several queries to compare the feasibility and usability of different environments. In the following paragraphs, you will find three examples.

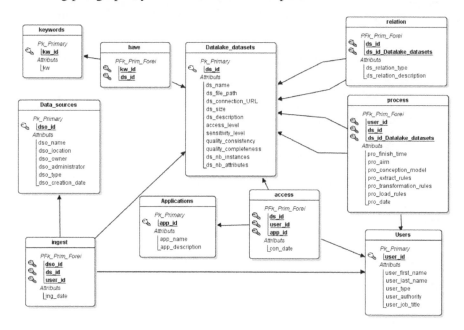

Figure 5.9. *Logical data model*

EXAMPLE 5.1.– When a user needs to work on a subject, they firstly need to find the dataset(s) that correspond to his requirement from all the datasets stored in the data lake. There is an example to find all the datasets related to the subject "brain trauma" to help users choose the dataset(s) that they will work on (see Figure 5.10).

EXAMPLE 5.2.– When a user finds the dataset they will work on, showing all the source datasets and target datasets (if they exist) of the chosen dataset is important to make the user gain more confidence in the data and to make their work easier. For example, the user in the first example will work on the dataset "OPTIMISME_TC" which is a data mart about brain trauma procedures. Now they want to know the source of the dataset "OPTIMISME_TC", if other datasets used the same source and if there is already some work based on the dataset "OPTIMISME_TC" (see Figure 5.11).

```
SELECT
    dd.ds_id,
    dd.ds_name,
    dd.ds_file_path,
    dd.ds_connection_url,
    dd.ds_size,
    dd.ds_description,
    dd.access_level,
    dd.sensitivity_level,
    dd.quality_completeness,
    dd.ds_nb_instance,
    dd.ds_nb_attributes,
    LISTAGG(kw.kw, ',') WITHIN GROUP (ORDER BY kw.kw) AS keywords
FROM
    datalake_datasets dd,
    keywords kw,
    have
WHERE
    dd.ds_id = have.ds_id
    AND have.kw_id = kw.kw_id
    AND (LOWER(kw.kw) LIKE '%brain%trauma%'
        OR LOWER(ds_description) LIKE '%brain%trauma%')
GROUP BY
    dd.ds_id,
    dd.ds_name,
    dd.ds_file_path,
    dd.ds_connection_url,
    dd.ds_size,
    dd.ds_description,
    dd.access_level,
    dd.sensitivity_level,
    dd.quality_completeness,
    dd.ds_nb_instance,
    dd.ds_nb_attributes;
```

Figure 5.10. *Request for finding all the datasets related to "brain trauma"*

EXAMPLE 5.3.– Users can also search for all datasets that have never been processed in the data lake to find a potential value from their data (see Figure 5.12).

```
SELECT
    ds_result.ds_id,
    ds_result.ds_name,
    ds_result.ds_file_path,
    ds_result.ds_connection_url,
    ds_result.ds_size,
    ds_result.ds_description,
    ds_result.access_level,
    ds_result.sensitivity_level,
    ds_result.quality_completeness,
    ds_result.ds_nb_instance,
    ds_result.ds_nb_attributes,
    LISTAGG(kw.kw, ',') WITHIN GROUP (ORDER BY kw.kw) AS keywords
FROM
    datalake_datasets ds_result,
    datalake_datasets ds,
    keywords kw,
    have,
    process
WHERE
    ds_result.ds_id = have.ds_id
    AND have.kw_id = kw.kw_id
    AND ds.ds_name = 'OPTIMISME_TC'
    /*find source data set with the next two joins*/
    AND ds.ds_id = process.ds_id
    AND ds_result.ds_id = process.ds_id_datalake_datasets
    /*find target data set with the next two joins*/
    AND ds.ds_id = process.ds_id_datalake_datasets
    AND ds_result.ds_id = process.ds_id
GROUP BY
    ds_result.ds_id,
    ds_result.ds_name,
    ds_result.ds_file_path,
    ds_result.ds_connection_url,
    ds_result.ds_size,
    ds_result.ds_description,
    ds_result.access_level,
    ds_result.sensitivity_level,
    ds_result.quality_completeness,
    ds_result.ds_nb_instance,
    ds_result.ds_nb_attributes;
```

Figure 5.11. *Request for finding source or target dataset*

5.4.2. *Graph database*

The second solution of implementation is graph database. We have chosen graph database because a data lake can contain a lot of raw datasets and processed sets; the relationships between all these datasets can be complex. Graph database can find many-to-many relationships efficiently [VIC 10], it

can help users find all the relevant datasets. To present the implementation of
the graph database, we first introduce a mapping between UML class diagram
and Neo4j model. Then a Neo4j model for the five datasets of UHC Toulouse
will be presented. In addition, two queries that answer the same questions in
the last section will be executed.

```
WITH processed_dataset AS(
    SELECT
        ds_id
    FROM
        datalake_datasets
    )

SELECT
    dd.ds_id,
    dd.ds_name,
    dd.ds_file_path,
    dd.ds_connection_url,
    dd.ds_size,
    dd.ds_description,
    dd.access_level,
    dd.sensitivity_level,
    dd.quality_completeness,
    dd.ds_nb_instance,
    dd.ds_nb_attributes,
    LISTAGG(kw.kw, ',') WITHIN GROUP (ORDER BY kw.kw) AS keywords
FROM
    datalake_datasets dd,
    keywords kw,
    have,
    processed_dataset pd
WHERE
    dd.ds_id = have.ds_id
    AND have.kw_id = kw.kw_id
    AND dd.ds_id IS NOT IN pd.ds_id
GROUP BY
    dd.ds_id,
    dd.ds_name,
    dd.ds_file_path,
    dd.ds_connection_url,
    dd.ds_size,
    dd.ds_description,
    dd.access_level,
    dd.sensitivity_level,
    dd.quality_completeness,
    dd.ds_nb_instance,
    dd.ds_nb_attributes;
```

Figure 5.12. *Request for finding all the datasets*
that have not been processed

To transform a relational database to a graph database, we extended a mapping from UML class diagram to property graphs [DEL 12] to Neo4j Cypher query language. We present different UML elements of the conceptual model by object diagram, property graph and Cypher languages. Note that Neo4j does not support bidirectional relationships and direction can be ignored while querying, so that for bidirectional association, only one direction needs to be created (see Figure 5.13).

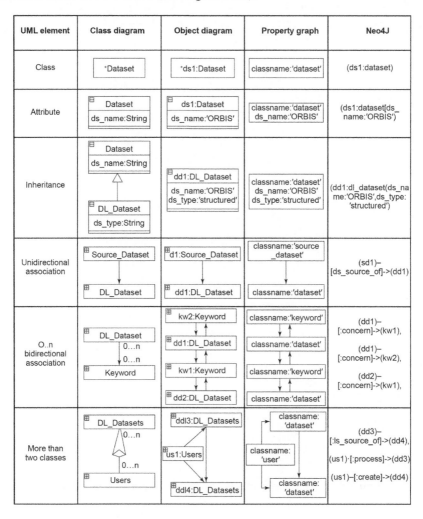

UML element	Class diagram	Object diagram	Property graph	Neo4J
Class	·Dataset	·ds1:Dataset	classname:'dataset'	(ds1:dataset)
Attribute	Dataset ds_name:String	ds1:Dataset ds_name:'ORBIS'	classname:'dataset' ds_name:'ORBIS'	(ds1:dataset[ds_ name:'ORBIS')
Inheritance	Dataset ds_name:String △ DL_Dataset ds_type:String	dd1:DL_Dataset ds_name:'ORBIS' ds_type:'structured'	classname:'dataset' ds_name:'ORBIS' ds_type:'structured'	(dd1:dl_dataset(ds_na me:'ORBIS',ds_type: 'structured')
Unidirectional association	Source_Dataset ↓ DL_Dataset	d1:Source_Dataset ↓ dd1:DL_Dataset	classname:'source _dataset' ↓ classname:'dataset'	(sd1)– [ds_source_of]->(dd1)
O..n bidirectional association	DL_Dataset 0...n 0...n Keyword	kw2:Keyword ↓↑ dd1:DL_Dataset ↓↑ kw1:Keyword ↑↓ dd2:DL_Dataset	classname:'keyword' ↓↑ classname:'dataset' ↓↑ classname:'keyword' ↑↓ classname:'dataset'	(dd1)– [:concern]->(kw1), (dd1)– [:concern]->(kw2), (dd2)– [:concern]->(kw1),
More than two classes	DL_Datasets △0...n 0...n Users	ddl3:DL_Datasets us1:Users ddl4:DL_Datasets	classname: 'dataset' classname: 'user' classname: 'dataset'	(dd3)– [:ls_source_of]->(dd4), (us1)·[:process]->(dd3) (us1)–[:create]->(dd4)

Figure 5.13. *Mapping between UML class diagram and Neo4J Cypher query language*

Based on the mapping, we implemented a graph database with neo4j (Figure 5.14). To test the implementation, we also answered the three questions (see Figure 5.15, Figure 5.16, Figure 5.18). Note that for the first question, we can also use a simple query to find not only the dataset(s) linked to a keyword but also all the other information linked to the dataset(s) (see Figure 5.17).

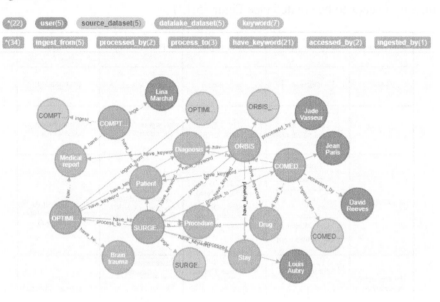

Figure 5.14. *Neo4j data model*

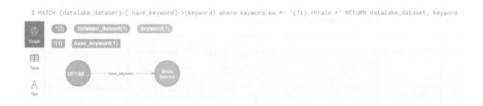

Figure 5.15. *Find the datasets concerning "brain trauma" – Neo4j*

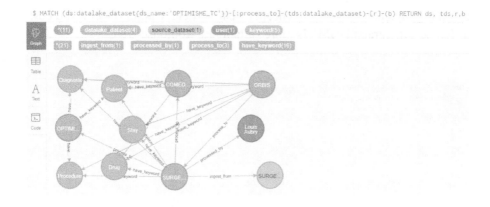

Figure 5.16. *Find the relevant dataset – Neo4j*

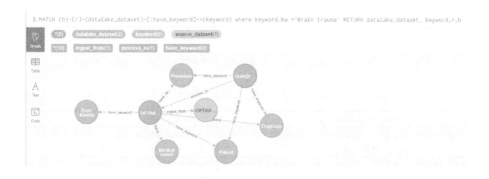

Figure 5.17. *Find the datasets concerning "brain trauma" and show all
the information linked to the datasets – Neo4j*

5.4.3. *Comparison of the solutions*

This section compares relational DBMS (database management system) with graph DBMS in terms of scalability, performance, flexibility, query language and security (see Table 5.2).

Scalability

RDBMSs use vertical scalability by adding computing power (CPU, RAM) to a machine [SAH 18]. In comparison, a graphical DBMS scales horizontally by adding machines, which is cheaper than vertical scaling. Due to the cost difference, the graph DBMS is more suitable for Toulouse UHC.

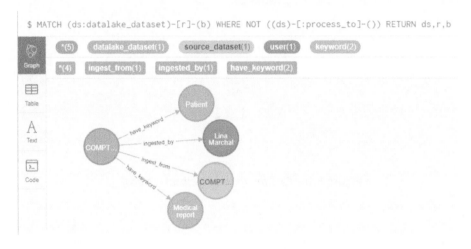

Figure 5.18. *Find the datasets that have not been processed – Neo4j*

	Relational DBMS	Graph DBMS
Scalability	Vertical scalability (volume growing with high cost)	Horizontal scalability (volume with low cost)
Flexibility	Modify database schema with lots of effort	Modify database schema with less effort
Query	Standard language. Complicated when there are many joins	Various languages. Easy to find related nodes
Security	Mature	Mature in some graph DBMSs

Table 5.2. *Comparison of relational and graph DBMS*

Flexibility

RDBMSs require predefined schema. Each modification of schema for an existing database may be costly, especially if the database has a complicated schema with many constraints [VIC 10]. Graph DBMS has more flexibility by using an agile and scalable model. After the experiment in Toulouse UHC, there was little addition in the conceptual model. Therefore, the metadata management system of UHC does not require high flexibility.

Query languages

Structured Query Language (SQL) is applied in different RDBMSs. Users can query by the common language in different systems. However, if databases are extended to adopt users' needs, SQL queries may be very complicated when there are numerous joins. With graph databases, queries can stay simple to find relations and relevant nodes. Nevertheless, different graph DBMSs use different query languages. The lack of standardization requires learning costs [MIL 13].

Security

RDBMSs have adopted mature mechanisms to make security certain. In RDBMSs, authentication is integrated, data integrity is ensured, communication is encrypted, auditing is provided [MOH 14]. Regarding graph DBMSs, some of them guarantee security services, for example, ArangoDB [STA 19a] and Neo4J [STA 19b]; some do not provide security mechanisms yet.

Given these different criteria, the UHC wishes to continue the experiment because the two types of DBMS have advantages and disadvantages. In addition, new sources may allow us to weigh a certain criteria so that we can choose the better system to manage metadata.

5.5. Concluding remarks

To prevent a data lake from turning into a data swamp, metadata management is recommended. In this chapter, we first proposed a generic and extensible classification of metadata with essential attributes adapted to the Toulouse UHC data lake project. The classification considers not only the metadata on each dataset (intra-metadata) but also the relationships between datasets (inter-metadata).

Based on the classification, we presented a conceptual model of metadata in data lakes. What is more, for validating the conception model, we implemented a graph DBMS and a relational DBMS for the metadata management system in the Toulouse UHC. The two solutions were tested by potential requirements. In addition, we compared graph and relational DBMS by four axes. The two DBMSs both have advantages and disadvantages, the decision of DBMS should be taken after considering the environment of implementation.

Our next plan concerns the automatic extraction of metadata. For this automatic extraction, we plan to integrate, into our existing work, the automatic detection of the relationships between the datasets [ALS 16], the data structure itself and the metadata characteristics. Nevertheless, no system can currently automatically extract inter-metadata and intra-metadata from different types (structured, semi-structured, unstructured) of datasets. What is more, the representation of our metadata model can evolve in time, for example, the form of ontology allows us to benefit from the reasoning engines and can establish an efficient link of our metadata with other external resources on the semantic web.

Our long term goal is to accomplish a metadata management system that integrates automatic extraction of data, effective research of metadata, automatic generation of dashboards or other analyses.

6

Master Data and Reference Data in Data Lake Ecosystems

The data lake relies more on the data-governance domain than the analytics domain in the information system. As data governance is key, such as the metadata strategy of avoiding the data lake to become a data swamp, the question is: what are the master data and reference data roles in the data lake architecture?

In this chapter, we first present the concepts of master data management (MDM) and reference data management, and then, we discuss their roles in the data lake concept and the values they bring.

Master data: according to the Gartner definition[1]: *Master data management is a technology-enabled discipline in which business and IT work together to ensure the uniformity, accuracy, stewardship, semantic consistency and accountability of the enterprise official shared master data assets. Master data is the consistent and uniform set of identifiers and extended attributes that describes the core entities of the enterprise including customers, prospects, citizens, suppliers, sites, hierarchies and chart of accounts.*

Reference data: *reference data refers to the data residing in code tables or lookup tables. They are normally static code tables storing values such as city and state codes, zip codes, product codes, country codes and industry*

Chapter written by Cédrine MADERA.

1 https://www.gartner.com/it-glossary/master-data-management-mdm/.

classification codes. Reference data has general characteristics. They are typically used in a read-only manner by operational, analytical and definitional systems. Reference data can be defined internally or specified externally by standards bodies groups (ISO, ANSI, etc.). Reference data can have a taxonomy, for example, hierarchy.

The data that is mastered may include[2]:

– reference data: the dimensions for analysis linked to business objects;

– master data: the business objects for transactions.

Figure 6.1 shows through an example of our definition of reference data, master data, metadata and transaction data.

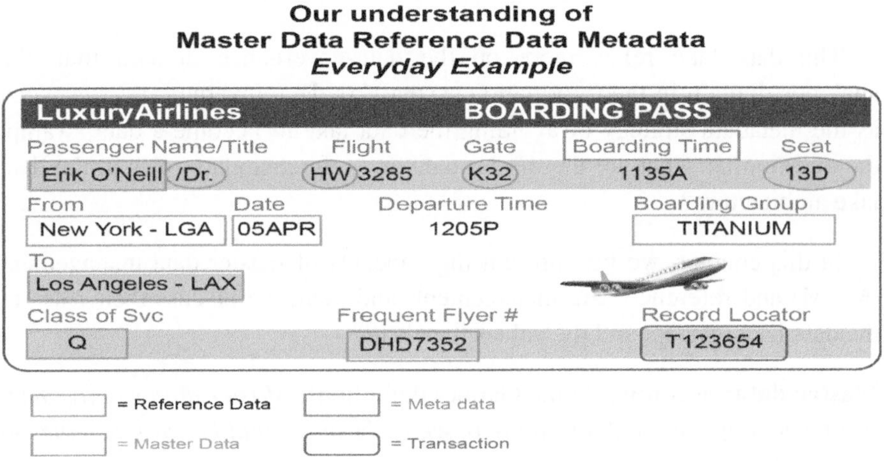

**Our understanding of
Master Data Reference Data Metadata
*Everyday Example***

Figure 6.1. *Illustration of master data, reference data and metadata.
For a color version of this figure, see www.iste.co.uk/laurent/data.zip*

This chapter gives a short overview on what MDM (including reference data management) is, why it is important and how one should manage it, while identifying some of the key MDM management patterns and best practices that are emerging.

---

2 From IBM Master data management view: http://www.redbooks.ibm.com/abstracts/sg248059. html?Open.

6.1. Introduction to master data management

The master data management (MDM) concept comes from organizations that are experiencing issues and difficulties around consistent reporting, regulatory compliance and all cross-projects based on data. This has prompted a great deal of interest in MDM.

6.1.1. *What is master data?*

Most software systems have lists of data that are shared and used by several of the applications that make up the system. For example, a typical ERP system as a minimum will have a customer master, an item master and an account master. This master data is often one of the key assets of a company. MDM provides a central repository of information on customers, assets, products, employees and so on, which is shared across several applications. MDM provides a single truth version of information.

6.1.2. *Basic definitions*

There are some very well-understood and easily identified master data items such as the *customer* and the *product*. In fact, many define master data by simply reciting a commonly agreed upon master data item list, such as customer, product, location, employee and asset. But how one identifies elements of data that should be managed by a master data management system is much more complex and defies such rudimentary definitions. In fact, there is a lot of confusion surrounding what master data is and how it is qualified, which calls for a more comprehensive treatment.

Data in corporations are mainly classified as follows:

– *Unstructured*: unstructured data is found in emails, raw documents, magazine articles, corporate intranet portals, product specifications, marketing collateral and PDF files.

– *Transactional*: transactional data is related to sales, deliveries, invoices, trouble tickets, claims and other monetary and non-monetary interactions.

– *Metadata*: metadata is data about other data and may reside in a formal repository or in various other forms such as XML documents, report definitions, column descriptions in a database, log files, connections and configuration files.

– *Hierarchical*: hierarchical data stores the relationships between other data. It may be stored as part of an accounting system or separately as descriptions of real-world relationships, such as company organizational structures or product lines. Hierarchical data is sometimes considered a super MDM domain, because it is critical to understanding and sometimes discovering the relationships between master data.

– *Master*: master data are the critical "nouns" of a business and generally fall into four groupings: people, things, places and concepts. Further categorizations within those groupings are called subject areas, domain areas or entity types. For example, within people, there are customers, employees and salespersons. Examples of things are products, parts, stores and assets. Examples of concepts are things like contracts, warranties and licenses.

Finally, within places, there are office locations and geographic divisions. Some of these domain areas may be further divided. The customer may be further segmented, based on incentives and history. A company may have normal customers, as well as premiere and executive customers. Products may be further segmented by sector and industry. The granularity of domains is essentially determined by the magnitude of differences between the attributes of the entities within them.

6.2. Deciding what to manage

While identifying master data entities is pretty straightforward, not all data that fit the definition for master data should necessarily be managed as such. This chapter narrows the definition of master data to the following criteria, all of which should be considered together when deciding if a given entity should be treated as master data or not[3].

6.2.1. *Behavior*

Master data can be described by the way it interacts with other data. For example, in transaction systems, master data is almost always involved with

---

3 https://www.ibm.com/analytics/master-data-management.

transactional data. A customer buys a product, a vendor sells a part and a partner delivers a crate of materials to a location. An employee is hierarchically related to their manager, who reports up through another manager (another employee). A product may be a part of multiple hierarchies describing their placement within a store. This relationship between master data and transactional data may be fundamentally viewed as a noun/verb relationship. Transactional data capture the verbs, such as sale, delivery, purchase, email and revocation; master data are the nouns. This is the same relationship data-warehouse facts and dimensions share.

6.2.2. Lifecycle

Master data can be described by the way that it is created, read, updated, deleted and searched. This lifecycle is called the CRUD[4] cycle and is different for different master data element types and companies. For example, how a customer is created largely depends on a company's business rules, industry segment and data systems. One company may have multiple customer-creation vectors, such as through the Internet, directly through account representatives or through outlet stores. Another company may only allow customers to be created through direct contact over the phone with its call center. Further, how a customer element is created is certainly different from how a vendor element is created.

6.2.3. Cardinality

As cardinality (the number of elements in a set) decreases, the likelihood of an element being treated as a master data element (even a commonly accepted subject area, such as the customer) decreases. For example, if a company only has three customers, most likely it would not consider those customers master data – at least, not in the context of supporting them with a master data management solution, simply because there is no benefit in managing those customers with a master data infrastructure. Yet, a company with thousands of customers would consider customer an important subject area because of the concomitant issues and benefits around managing such a

---

4 CRUD: created, read, updated, deleted.

large set of entities. The customer value to each of these companies is the same. Both rely upon their customers for business. One needs a customer master data solution, while the other does not. Cardinality does not change the classification of a given entity type; however, the importance of having a solution for managing an entity type increases as the cardinality of the entity type increases.

6.2.4. *Lifetime*

Master data tends to be less volatile than transactional data. As it becomes more volatile, it is typically considered more transactional. For example, some might consider a *contract* as a master data element, while others might consider it a transaction. Depending on the lifespan of a contract, it can go either way. An agency promoting professional sportspersons might consider their contracts as master data. Each is different from the other and typically has a lifetime longer than a year. It may be tempting to simply have one master data item called *sportsperson*. However, athletes tend to have more than one contract at any given time: one with their teams and others with companies for endorsing products. The agency would need to manage all those contracts over time, as elements of the contract are renegotiated or sportspersons are traded. Other contracts, for example, contracts for detailing cars or painting a house, are more like a transaction. They are one-time, short-lived agreements to provide services for payment and are typically fulfilled and destroyed within hours.

6.2.5. *Complexity*

Simple entities, even valuable entities, are rarely a challenge to manage and are rarely considered master data elements. The less complex an element, the less likely the need to manage change for that element. Typically, such assets are simply collected and tallied.

6.2.6. *Value*

The more valuable the data element is to the company, the more likely it will be considered a master data element. Value and complexity work together.

6.2.7. *Volatility*

While master data is typically less volatile than transactional data, entities with attributes that do not change at all typically do not require a master data solution. For example, rare coins would seem to meet many of the criteria for a master data treatment. A rare-coin collector would likely have many rare coins. So, cardinality is high. They are valuable. They are also complex. For example, rare coins have a history and description. There are attributes, such as condition of obverse, reverse, legend, inscription, rim and field. There are other attributes, such as designer initials, edge design, layers and portrait. Yet, rare coins do not need to be managed as a master data item, because they do not change over time or, at least, they do not change enough. There may need to be more information added, as the history of a particular coin is revealed or if certain attributes must be corrected. But, generally speaking, rare coins would not be managed through a master data management system, because they are not volatile enough to warrant a solution.

6.2.8. *Reuse*

One of the primary drivers of master data management is reuse. For example, in a simple world, the CRM system would manage everything about a customer and never need to share any information about the customer with other systems. However, in today's complex environments, customer information needs to be shared across multiple applications. That is where the trouble begins. Because for a number of reasons, access to a master datum is not always available, people start storing master data in various locations, such as spreadsheets and application private stores. There are still reasons, such as data quality degradation and decay, to manage master data that is not reused across the enterprise. However, if a master data entity is reused in multiple systems, it should be managed with a master data management system.

To summarize, while it is simple to enumerate the various master data entity types, it is sometimes more challenging to decide which data items in a company should be treated as master data. Often, data that does not normally comply with the definition for master data may need to be managed as such, and data that does comply with the definition may not. Ultimately, when deciding on what entity types should be treated as master data, it is better to categorize them in terms of their behavior and attributes within the context of the business' needs rather than to rely on simple lists of entity types.

6.3. Why should I manage master data?

Since it is used by multiple applications, an error in master data can cause errors in all the applications that use it. For example, an incorrect address in the customer master might mean orders, bills and marketing literature are all sent to the wrong address. Similarly, an incorrect price on an item master can be a marketing disaster, and an incorrect account number in an account master can lead to huge problems.

Even if the master data has no errors, few organizations have just one set of master data. Many companies grow through mergers and acquisitions. Each company you acquire comes with its own customer master, item master and so forth. This would not be bad if you could just Union the new master data with your current master data, but unless the company you acquire is in a completely different business in a faraway country, there is a very good chance that some customers and products will appear in both sets of master data – usually with different formats and different database keys.

If both companies use the Social Security number as the customer identifier, discovering which customer records are for the same customer is straightforward; but that seldom happens. In most cases, customer numbers and part numbers are assigned by the software that creates the master records, so the chances of the same customer or the same product having the same identifier in both databases is pretty remote. Item masters can be even harder to reconcile, if equivalent parts are purchased from different vendors with different vendor numbers.

Merging master lists together can be very difficult. The same customer may have different names, customer numbers, addresses and phone numbers in different databases. For example, William Smith might appear as Bill Smith, Wm. Smith and William Smithe. Normal database joins and searches will not be able to resolve these differences. A very sophisticated tool that understands nicknames, alternate spellings and typing errors will be required. The tool will probably also have to recognize that different name variations can be resolved, if they all live at the same address or have the same phone number. While creating a clean master list can be a daunting challenge, there are many positive benefits to your bottom line from a common master list:

– a single, consolidated bill saves money and improves customer satisfaction;

– sending the same marketing literature to a customer from multiple customer lists wastes money and irritates the customer;

– before you turn a customer account over to a collection agency, it would be good to know if they owe other parts of your company money or, more importantly, that they are another division's biggest customer;

– stocking the same item under different part numbers is not only a waste of money and shelf space but can potentially lead to artificial shortages.

The recent movements towards data platform render master data management a critical issue. For example, if you create a single customer service that communicates through well-defined XML messages, you may think you have defined a single view of your customers. However, if the same customer is stored in five databases with three different addresses and four different phone numbers, then what will your customer service return? Similarly, if you decide to subscribe to a CRM service provided through SaaS, the service provider will need a list of customers for their database. Which one will you send them?

For all these reasons, maintaining a high-quality, consistent set of master data for your organization is rapidly becoming a necessity. The systems and processes required to maintain this data are known as master data management.

6.4. What is master data management?

For purposes of this chapter, we define master data management (MDM) as the technology, tools and processes required to create and maintain consistent and accurate lists of master data. There are a couple of things worth noting in this definition. One is that MDM is not just a technological problem. In many cases, fundamental changes to a business process will be required to maintain clean master data, and some of the most difficult MDM issues are more political than technical. The second thing to note is that MDM includes both creating and maintaining master data. Investing a lot of time, money and effort in creating a clean, consistent set of master data is a wasted effort unless the solution includes tools and processes to keep the master data clean and consistent as it gets updated and expanded.

While MDM is most effective when applied to all the master data in an organization, in many cases, the risk and expense of an enterprise-wide effort are difficult to justify. It may be easier to start with a few key sources of master data and expand the effort, once success has been demonstrated and lessons have been learned. If you do start small, you should include an analysis of all the master data that you might eventually want to include, so you do not make design decisions or tool choices that will force you to start over when you try to incorporate a new data source. For example, if your initial customer master implementation only includes the 10,000 customers your direct sales force deals with, you do not want to make design decisions that will preclude adding your 10,000,000 web customers later.

An MDM project plan will be influenced by requirements, priorities, resource availability, time frame and the size of the problem. Most MDM projects include at least these phases:

1) *Identify sources of master data.* This step is usually a very revealing exercise. Some companies find they have dozens of databases containing customer data that the IT department did not know existed.

2) *Identify the producers and consumers of the master data.* It is difficult to determine which applications produce the master data identified in the first step, and generally, it is more difficult to determine which applications use the master data. Depending on the approach you use for maintaining the master data, this step might not be necessary. For example, if all changes are detected and handled at the database level, it probably does not matter where the changes come from.

3) *Collect and analyze metadata about your master data.* For all the sources identified in step one, what are the entities and attributes of the data and what do they mean? This should include attribute name, datatype, allowed values, constraints, default values, dependencies and who owns the definition and maintenance of the data. The owner is the most important and often the hardest to determine. If you have a repository loaded with all your metadata, this step is an easy one. If you have to start from database tables and source code, this could be a significant effort.

4) *Appoint data stewards*. These are the people with the knowledge of the current source data and the ability to determine how to transform the source into the master data format. In general, stewards should be appointed from the owners of each master data source, the architects responsible for the MDM systems and representatives from the business users of the master data.

5) *Implement a data-governance program and data-governance council.* This group must have the knowledge and authority to make decisions on how the master data is maintained, what it contains, how long it is kept, and how changes are authorized and audited. Hundreds of decisions must be made in the course of a master data project, and if there is not a well-defined decision-making body and process, the project can fail, because the politics prevent effective decision-making.

6) *Develop the master data model*. Decide what the master records look like: what attributes are included, what size and datatype they are, what values are allowed and so forth. This step should also include the mapping between the master data model and the current data sources. This is usually both the most important and most difficult step in the process. If you try to make everybody happy by including all the source attributes in the master entity, you often end up with master data that is too complex and cumbersome to be useful. For example, if you cannot decide whether weight should be in pounds or kilograms, one approach would be to include both (Weight Lb and Weight Kg). While this might make people happy, you are wasting megabytes of storage for numbers that can be calculated in microseconds, as well as running the risk of creating inconsistent data (Weight Lb = 5 and Weight Kg = 5). While this is a pretty trivial example, a bigger issue would be maintaining multiple part numbers for the same part. As in any committee effort, there will be fights and deals resulting in sub-optimal decisions. It is important to work out the decision process, priorities and final decision-maker in advance, to make sure things run smoothly.

7) *Choose a tool set*. You will need to buy or build tools to create the master lists by cleaning, transforming and merging the source data. You will also need an infrastructure to use and maintain the master list. You can use a single tool set from a single vendor for all of these functions, or you might want to take a best-of-breed approach. In general, the techniques to clean and merge data are different for different types of data, so there are not a lot of tools that span the whole range of master data. The two main categories of tools are customer data integration (CDI) tools for creating the customer master and

product information management (PIM) tools for creating the product master. Some tools will do both, but generally they are better at one or the other.

The tool set should also have support for finding and fixing data quality issues and maintaining versions and hierarchies. Versioning is a critical feature, because understanding the history of a master data record is vital to maintaining its quality and accuracy over time. For example, if a merge tool combines two records for John Smith in Boston, and you decide there really are two different John Smiths in Boston, you need to know what the records looked like before they were merged in order to *unmerge* them.

8) *Design the infrastructure.* Once you have clean, consistent master data, you will need to expose it to your applications and provide processes to manage and maintain it. When this infrastructure is implemented, you will have a number of applications that will depend on it being available, so reliability and scalability are important considerations to include in your design. In most cases, you will have to implement significant parts of the infrastructure yourself, because it will be designed to fit into your current infrastructure, platforms and applications.

9) *Generate and test the master data.* This step is where you use the tools you have developed or purchased to merge your source data into your master data list. This is often an iterative process requiring tinkering with rules and settings to get the matching right. This process also requires a lot of manual inspection to ensure that the results are correct and meet the requirements established for the project. No tool will get the matching done correctly 100% of the time, so you will have to weigh the consequences of false matches versus missed matches to determine how to configure the matching tools. False matches can lead to customer dissatisfaction, if bills are inaccurate or the wrong person is arrested. Too many missed matches make the master data less useful, because you are not getting the benefits you invested in MDM to get.

10) *Modify the producing and consuming systems.* Depending on how your MDM implementation is designed, you might have to change the systems that produce, maintain or consume master data to work with the new source of master data. If the master data is used in a system separate from the source systems, a data warehouse, for example, the source systems might not have to change. If the source systems are going to use the master data, however, changes will likely be required. Either the source systems will have to access

the new master data or the master data will have to be synchronized with the source systems, so that the source systems have a copy of the cleaned up master data to use. If it is not possible to change one or more of the source systems, either that source system might not be able to use the master data or the master data will have to be integrated with the source system's database through external processes, such as triggers and SQL commands.

The source systems generating new records should be changed to look up existing master record sets before creating new records or updating existing master records. This ensures that the quality of data being generated upstream is good, so that the MDM can function more efficiently and the application itself manages data quality. MDM should be leveraged not only as a system of record but also as an application that promotes cleaner and more efficient handling of data across all applications in the enterprise. As part of the MDM strategy, all three pillars of data management need to be looked into: data origination, data management and data consumption. It is not possible to have a robust enterprise-level MDM strategy if any one of these aspects is ignored.

11) *Implement the maintenance processes.* As we stated earlier, any MDM implementation must incorporate tools, processes and people to maintain the quality of the data. All data must have a data steward who is responsible for ensuring the quality of the master data. The data steward is normally a businessperson who has knowledge of the data, can recognize incorrect data and has the knowledge and authority to correct the issues. The MDM infrastructure should include tools that help the data steward recognize issues and simplify corrections. A good data stewardship tool should point out questionable matches between customers with different names and customer numbers that live at the same address, for example. The steward might also want to review items that were added as new, because the match criteria were close but below the threshold. It is important for the data steward to see the history of changes made to the data by the MDM systems, to isolate the source of errors and to undo incorrect changes. Maintenance also includes the processes to pull changes and additions into the MDM system and to distribute the cleansed data to the required places.

As you can see, MDM is a complex process that can go on for a long time. Like most things in software, the key to success is to implement MDM incrementally so that the business realizes a series of short-term benefits while the complete project is a long-term process. No MDM project can be successful without the support and participation of the business users. IT professionals do not have the domain knowledge to create and maintain high-quality master data.

Any MDM project that does not include changes to the processes that create, maintain and validate master data is likely to fail. The rest of this chapter will cover the details of the technology and processes for creating and maintaining master data.

6.4.1. *How do I create a master list?*

Whether you buy a tool or decide to create your own, there are two basic steps to create master data: clean and standardize the data and match data from all the sources to consolidate duplicates. Before you can start cleaning and normalizing your data, you must understand the data model for the master data. As part of the modeling process, the contents of each attribute were defined, and a mapping was defined from each source system to the master data model. This information is used to define the transformations necessary to clean your source data.

Cleaning the data and transforming it into the master data model is very similar to the extract, transform and load (ETL) processes used to populate a data warehouse. If you already have ETL tools and transformation defined, it might be easier to simply modify these as required for the master data, instead of learning a new tool. Here are some typical data cleansing functions:

– Normalize data formats: make all the phone numbers look the same, transform addresses (and so on) to a common format.

– Replace missing values: insert defaults, look up ZIP codes from the address, look up the Dun and Bradstreet number.

– Standardize values: convert all measurements to metric, convert prices to a common currency, change part numbers to an industry standard.

– Map attributes: parse the first name and the last name out of a contact-name field, move Part and partno to the PartNumber field.

Most tools will cleanse the data that they can and put the rest into an error table for hand processing. Depending on how the matching tool works, the cleansed data will be put into a master table or a series of staging tables. As each source is cleansed, the output should be examined to ensure the cleansing process is working correctly.

Matching master data records to eliminate duplicates is both the hardest and most important step in creating master data. False matches can actually lose data (two XYZ corporations become one, for example), and missed matches reduce the value of maintaining a common list. The matching accuracy of MDM tools is one of the most important purchase criteria. Some matches are pretty trivial to carry out.

If you have Social Security numbers for all your customers, or if all your products use a common numbering scheme, a database JOIN will find most of the matches. This hardly ever happens in the real world, however, so matching algorithms are normally very complex and sophisticated. Customers can be matched on name, maiden name, nickname, address, phone number, credit card number and so on, while products are matched on name, description, part number, specifications and price. The more attribute matches and the closer the match, the higher degree of confidence the MDM system has in the match. This confidence factor is computed for each match, and if it surpasses a threshold, the records match. The threshold is normally adjusted depending on the consequences of a false match. For example, you might specify that if the confidence level is over 95%, the records are merged automatically, and if the confidence is between 80 and 95%, a data steward should approve the match before they are merged.

Most merge tools merge one set of input into the master list, so the best procedure is to start the list with the data in which you have the most confidence, and then merge the other sources in one at a time. If you have a lot of data and a lot of problems with it, this process can take a long time. You might want to start with the data from which you expect to get the most benefit having consolidated; run a pilot project with that data to ensure your processes work and you are seeing the business benefits you expect; and then start adding other sources, as time and resources permit. This approach means your project will take longer and possibly cost more, but the rate of risk is lower. This approach also lets you start with a few organizations and add more as the project becomes more successful, instead of trying to get everybody onboard from the start.

Another factor to consider when merging your source data into the master list is privacy. When customers become part of the customer master, their information might be visible to any of the applications that have access to the customer master. If the customer data was obtained under a privacy policy that limited its use to a particular application, then you might not be able to merge it into the customer master. You might want to add a lawyer to your MDM planning team.

6.4.2. *How do I maintain a master list?*

There are many different tools and techniques for managing and using master data. We will cover three of the more common scenarios here:

– *Single-copy approach.* In this approach, there is only one master copy of the master data. All additions and changes are made directly to the master data. All applications that use master data are rewritten to use the new data instead of their current data. This approach guarantees consistency of the master data, but in most cases, it is not practical. Modifying all your applications to use a new data source with a different schema and different data is, at least, very expensive; if some of your applications are purchased, it might even be impossible.

– *Multiple copies, single maintenance.* In this approach, master data is added or changed in the single master copy of the data, but changes are sent out to the source systems in which copies are stored locally. Each application can update the parts of the data that are not part of the master data, but they cannot change or add master data. For example, the inventory system might be able to change quantities and locations of parts, but new parts cannot be added, and the attributes that are included in the product master cannot be changed. This reduces the number of application changes that will be required, but the applications will minimally have to disable functions that add or update master data. Users will have to learn new applications to add or modify master data, and some of the things they normally do will not work anymore.

– *Continuous merge.* In this approach, applications are allowed to change their copy of the master data. Changes made to the source data are sent to the master, where they are merged into the master list. The changes to the master are then sent to the source systems and applied to the local copies. This approach requires few changes to the source systems; if necessary, the change propagation can be handled in the database, so no application code is changed.

On the surface, this seems like the ideal solution. Application changes are minimized, and no retraining is required. Everybody keeps doing what they are doing, but with higher quality, more complete data. This approach does however have several issues.

- Update conflicts are possible and difficult to reconcile. What happens if two of the source systems change a customer's address to different values? There is no way for the MDM system to decide which one to keep, so intervention by the data steward is required; in the meantime, the customer has two different addresses. This must be addressed by creating data-governance rules and standard operating procedures, to ensure that update conflicts are reduced or eliminated.

- Additions must be remerged. When a customer is added, there is a chance that another system has already added the customer. To deal with this situation, all data additions must go through the matching process again to prevent new duplicates in the master.

- Maintaining consistent values is more difficult. If the weight of a product is converted from pounds to kilograms and then back to pounds, rounding can change the original weight. This can be disconcerting to a user who enters a value and then sees it change a few seconds later.

In general, all these things can be planned for and dealt with, making the user's life a little easier, at the expense of a more complicated infrastructure to maintain and more work for the data stewards. This might be an acceptable trade-off, but it is one that should be made consciously.

6.4.3. *Versioning and auditing*

No matter how you manage your master data, it is important to be able to understand how the data got to the current state. For example, if a customer record was consolidated from two different merged records, you might need to know what the original records looked like, in case a data steward determines that the records were merged by mistake and they really should be two different customers.

The version management should include a simple interface for displaying versions and reverting all or part of a change to a previous version. The normal branching of versions and grouping of changes that source-control systems use can also be very useful for maintaining different derivation changes and reverting groups of changes to a previous branch.

Data stewardship and compliance requirements will often include a way to determine who made each change and when it was made. To support these requirements, an MDM system should include a facility for auditing changes to the master data. In addition to keeping an audit log, the MDM system should include a simple way to find the particular change you are looking for. An MDM system can audit thousands of changes a day, so search and reporting facilities for the audit log are important.

6.4.4. *Hierarchy management*

In addition to the master data itself, the MDM system must maintain data hierarchies, for example, a bill of materials for products, sales territory structure, organization structure for customers and so forth. It is important for the MDM system to capture these hierarchies, but it is also useful for an MDM system to be able to modify the hierarchies independently of the underlying systems. For example, when an employee moves to a different cost center, there might be impacts to the travel and expense system, payroll, time reporting, reporting structures and performance management.

If the MDM system manages hierarchies, a change to the hierarchy in a single place can propagate the change to all the underlying systems. There might also be reasons to maintain hierarchies in the MDM system that do not exist in the source systems. For example, revenue and expenses might need to be rolled up into territory or organizational structures that do not exist in any single source system. Planning and forecasting might also require temporary hierarchies to calculate *what if* numbers for proposed organizational changes. Historical hierarchies are also required in many cases to roll up financial information into structures that existed in the past, but not in the current structure. For these reasons, a powerful, flexible hierarchy management feature is an important part of an MDM system.

The recent emphasis on regulatory compliance and mergers and acquisitions has made the creation and maintaining of accurate and complete master data a business imperative. Both large and small businesses must develop data-maintenance and data-governance processes and procedures, to obtain and maintain accurate master data. The Big Data wave with the data lake strong adoption and its position as one of the main components of the information system can benefit from this master data environment to improve the data quality of the expected insights.

The next section deals with the relationship between data lake and MDM.

6.5. Master data and the data lake

Master data can deliver the same benefits in the data lake that it has delivered for years in more traditional data stores: eliminating inconsistency, resolving duplicates and creating a single version of the truth. It also manages the relationships between master data.

There are two ways to master data in a data lake:

– feeding mastered data into the lake from the MDM hub;

– mastering data in the data lake itself.

In the first approach, companies use an MDM hub to master the data. The MDM hub improves the quality of core data that is fed into the data lake.

In the second approach, companies that have an extraordinarily high number of records can master the data within the data lake itself. This frees up data scientists to spend more time exploring and analyzing, and less time trying to fix data issues, such as duplicate customer records. It also helps data scientists understand the relationships between the data; to see all members of a household, for example.

Figures 6.2 and 6.3 point out the architecture pain points within the relationship between MDM and the data lake:

– scenario 1: MDM is external to the data lake;

– scenario 2: MDM is internal to the data lake.

The choice between scenario 1 with MDM external and scenario 2 with MDM integrated to the data lake will depend on different factors such as:

– existing MDM strategy and tooling in place and usage;

– data lake ongoing construction;

– data lake position in the data strategy.

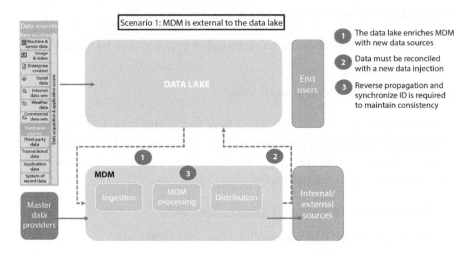

Figure 6.2. *Scenario 1: MDM hub*

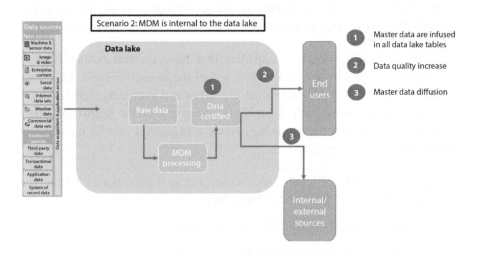

Figure 6.3. *Scenario 2: MDM in the data lake*

Other factors can also influence the choice between scenarios 1 and 2 and will depend on the data lake maturity and usage. For organization which already have an MDM strategy in place, scenario 1 will be the best option. For organizations which do not yet have an MDM solution in place, starting with MDM placement like in scenario 2 is a good option to improve data governance. In any case, the master data component is an essential piece of the information system, which must be connected to the data lake environment and being leverage[5].

6.6. Conclusion

In metadata management, the master data management is an important part of the data governance strategy. The data lake adoption will depend on the way those two main components are involved in the data lake architecture design. Without a metadata strategy, the data lake can become a data swamp; without a good leverage of the MDM part, the data lake can become a distrusted data platform.

---

5 Article on MDM data hub: https://www.linkedin.com/pulse/why-centralized-master-data-management-strategy-going-cedrine-madera/.

7

Linked Data Principles for Data Lakes

Linked Data are based on a set of principles and technologies to exploit the architecture of the Web in order to represent and provide access to machine-readable, globally integrated information. Those principles and technologies have many advantages when applied in the context of implementing data lakes, both generally and in particular domains.

This chapter provides an overview of what Linked Data means, and of the general approach to create and consume Linked Data resources. It is shown how this approach can be used at different levels in a data lake, including basic graph-based data storage and querying, data integration and data cataloging. To exemplify the application of Linked Data principles and technologies for data lakes, a demonstrating scenario is given in the context of the creation and application of a large data platform for a smart city: the MK Data Hub.

7.1. Basic principles

The simplest notion of *Linked Data*, as indicated in this capitalized case, is that of a *paradigm* for representing and publishing data of any kind: a paradigm that is comprised of a set of design principles, which are, in turn, supported by a set of core technologies. If someone publishes a dataset and in so doing:

– uses unique identifiers to reference each entity in the data;

– makes it possible for those identifiers to be looked up by anyone;

Chapter written by Alessandro ADAMOU and Mathieu D'AQUIN..

– uses standards to represent the information that is returned by looking up those identifiers;

– or ensures that the information references other things by their identifiers where applicable;

then it can be said that those data are published in accordance with the Linked Data principles [BER 09]; such data may therefore be called *linked data*.

While the aforementioned items can be seen as general principles for implementing a semantically rich platform for managing data, there is a reasonably well-defined instantiation of this philosophy, which comes in the form of recommended formats and languages. The four criteria have been standardized into a technology stack that provides guidelines for their fulfilment:

1) Unique Resource Identifiers (URIs) are used as the basic identification mechanism of all entities, or *resources*.

2) In particular, the guidelines suggest that HTTP URLs should be used whenever possible as identifiers, as there are ways for everyone to look them up, or *dereference* them.

3) HTTP clients, including but not limited to Web browsers, abound to that end. A few standards have been selected, such as the Resource Description Framework (RDF), a minimal yet powerful representation mechanism based on the syntactic metaphor of subject-predicate-object, and as the SPARQL language, a publicly accessible interface for querying linked data.

4) The fourth criterion suggests that the *values* in a linked dataset should not be limited to strings or numbers, but should also include URIs that identify other things, whose information is in turn represented according to the same principles.

Among the quality criteria for datasets published as linked data is the notion of reuse. Reusing data according to the fourth of the above criteria may be regarded much like the practice of adopting foreign keys in traditional relational databases, except that the notion extends far beyond the assumed closed worlds of relational databases.

On a Web scale, anything that is an identifiable entity with a machine-readable description on the Web is a good candidate for being referenced: if, for instance, someone has already formalized in some way a notion of France, an airplane or Ludwig van Beethoven, there is no reason to recreate this notion, as the existing one can be referenced instead.

If reuse is encouraged for already represented things, then this is even truer for the *vocabularies* used for representing their information. Since URIs are also used for predicates such as "birthplace", "was composed by", "is a" etc., proposing such predicates as standards and reusing them is a helpful practice towards a common way of understanding the data published by third parties. This gives rise to a particular discipline in knowledge engineering, i.e. the creation of *controlled vocabularies* (taxonomies, thesauri) and *ontologies*, which can be used and combined so as to form the *schemas* for the data being published. Some common RDF properties that represent the above examples are <http://d-nb.info/standards/elementset/gnd#placeOfBirth> for 'birthplace' (from the "Gemeinsame Normdatei" Integrated Authority File Ontology), <http://purl.org/ontology/mo/composer> for 'was composed by' (from the Music Ontology), and <http://www.w3.org/1999/02/22-rdf-syntax-ns#type> for 'is a' (the default RDF property for types of things).

Other key features of Linked Data that are highlighted here in view of their applicability to data lakes are:

– *Open world assumption*: unlike the closed world of *data silos*, where every statement that is not explicitly true is considered false, if a fact is not present in the information returned when we dereference a Linked Data resource, then it is not considered to be false. This is because this fact might not have been discovered yet or taken into consideration. Another dataset reusing that resource could then state that the fact is true.

– *Monotonicity*: owing to the open world assumption, information is only provided by stating new facts about an entity. Facts are always added, never subtracted or voided by other facts. However, they can be contradicted by the addition of facts, which can generate logical inconsistencies, which in turn need to be dealt with.

– *Representational ambivalence*: Linked Data is a paradigm that applies to data publishing and storage in near-equal capacities. While the recommendations and methodologies mostly affect the former, they also provide indications on dealing with the latter. In particular, data linking and vocabulary reuse are two characteristics that encourage people to store data using the same schema and format (i.e. triples or quadruples, regardless of the specific serialization format) as the ones used for publishing them [HAR 12].

The above synthetically illustrated principles of open world assumption, monotonicity and representational ambivalence, offer several insights as to how the Linked Data paradigm lends itself to the flexibility assumed for data lakes. In the following, a set of practices and common techniques for achieving this flexibility will be described, along with a few example applications.

7.2. Using Linked Data in data lakes

Both Linked Data and data lakes operate under principles that could be interpreted as an assumption of levity towards the traditional rigor of database systems: in Linked Data, because the addition of new triples using new properties implies a lightweight alteration of the schema; in Data Lakes, because the way in which data are stored generally disregards the potential for future use. In the following, we shall argue that this perceived laxity would be a misconception, as it can be shown how, if we interpret it as flexibility towards certain dimensions, it actually allows the two paradigms to interoperate. In other words, Linked Data principles can overcome the perceived rigor of traditional databases, not because they want to be lacking in such rigor, but because it is regarded as an overkill, as a Linked Data-based data space has a way of naturally establishing strong relationships. Particularly, this section will present three areas where the principles and technologies of Linked Data find fertile ground for application to data lakes. These are: (1) storage and querying (both low-level and through public query interfaces); (2) data integration, within a system or across systems and (3) data cataloging and profiling.

Let us recall that one basic characteristic of data lakes is that the data are stored in their original source form, and are therefore made readily available for querying in such a form. This may be regarded as an advantage because a data lake structured in this way can be generated fairly quickly with minimum transformation overhead: it will be possible to defer data analytics to a significantly later time, whereupon the data are transformed and cleaned once the users have a clear idea as to what to do with them.

The controversy that looms around the data lake paradigm, on the other hand, concerns exactly this latter aspect. One criticism against data lakes is that, in order to be exploitable, a data lake requires or assumes a degree of knowledge on the consumers' part of the context and processes behind the ingestion of those data, and this information is likely to be lost or not recorded at data generation time. In other words, by looking at the data alone, one would hardly be able to infer the proper ways in which different datasets should be used together.

The Linked Data principles have a way of mitigating this drawback. For one thing, while there exists a notion of dataset in Linked Data, it is a very loose one, in that the granularity of a dataset may be associated to that of an RDF graph or a set of one or more graphs that can be accessed through the same service endpoint for querying (in the SPARQL language). A consequence of this is that, given a mass of linked data, it is possible to logically partition it into datasets without fundamentally altering the structure and semantics of its content.

However, a dataset shaped in this way can be annotated with metadata that aid their interpretation by human users, such as provenance information. The granularity of this logical partitioning can therefore be tuned to accommodate the information that the creators deem sufficient to characterize each part with an identity, distinct provenance and documentation.

For example, suppose that an archaeological linked dataset catalogs all the Roman inscriptions in Latin[1]. The fact that the inscriptions are in Latin is not encoded in the data itself, for each inscription, but inside a data unit in the metadata for the whole dataset – seen as such due to being accessible via its own SPARQL endpoint. If the content of such a dataset were to be made part of a larger archaeological data lake, this information is likely to be lost along with the metadata. If, however, the data of every inscription were directly annotated with this information, not only would that give them a stronger semantic characterization (after all, language is an intrinsic characteristic of

---

1 See, for example, the Epigraphic Database Heidelberg: https://edh-www.adw.uni-heidelberg.de/data/.

inscriptions and one should know the language of an inscription by looking at its data alone), but also it would reduce their dependency on metadata: hence the rule of thumb of encoding as much information as possible in the data.

However, as importantly as with dataset granularity, let us recall that the Linked Data paradigm is valid for data storage as well as for publishing. Consequently, the fourth principle of reuse mentioned earlier in this chapter, once applied to data vocabularies, can be implemented at the time of generating and storing the data on a bare-metal storage platform. If the vocabularies being reused are standardized or at least widespread, the burden of interpreting the data at a later time can be significantly reduced.

A number of cross-domain vocabularies can be used to keep the adoption bar low when describing entities whose semantics are valid across multiple domains, such as physical agents (e.g. FOAF[2]), published work (DCMI[3]), social media (SIOC[4] and again FOAF), sensor networks (SSN[5]) or statistical observations over a domain (DataCube[6]). These are all heavily adopted open standards with globally understood semantics which, coupled with a variety of documented domain ontologies (covering, for example, education, cultural heritage or music[7]) make it possible – or at least much easier – to semantically interpret at a later stage the data that conform to them.

Not only is the notion of a dataset a rather lax one, it also almost exclusively concerns the meta-level. Ideally, the Web of Data would be a single, all-comprising dataset where every fact that is stated represents a truth that holds regardless of the context of where that fact sits. The partitioning of the Web of Data into datasets is an artifice that comes from the need to address concerns that affect the usage of the data, not the data itself. Examples include: data authorship, license to use, ownership, change history, responsibilities, quality of service and, ultimately, whether or not the stated facts can be trusted. Indeed, trust and provenance are among the issues that

---

2 Friend-Of-A-Friend namespace document: http://xmlns.com/foaf/spec/.

3 Dublin Core Metadata Initiative: http://dublincore.org/documents/dcmi-terms/.

4 Semantically Interlinked Online Communities: http://rdfs.org/sioc/spec/.

5 Semantic Sensor Network Ontology: https://www.w3.org/TR/vocab-ssn/.

6 RDF Data Cube Vocabulary: https://www.w3.org/TR/vocab-data-cube/.

7 See also Linked Open Vocabularies (LOV) [VAN 17] for a comprehensive set of reusable data vocabularies: https://lov.okfn.org/dataset/lov/vocabs.

keep the Web of Linked Data from being regarded as a data lake. The underlying logic, however, allows a potentially seamless integration of these data.

A similar principle holds for Web ontologies. An ontology is a formal representation of a domain, and is comprised of terms like types and properties. These terms are then employed for assembling the *schema* of a linked dataset. As reuse is an important factor in the construction of data networks, and even more so when the material being reused is the terms used to describe the data. Ontologies can be regarded as linked datasets by their own right, whose core content is the terms used to lay out the logical framework.

When a knowledge engineer and a dataset author agree to use a subset of terms, such as classes and properties, from an ontology, they are not necessarily committing to cover the entire ontology with their data. More often than not, they will instead resort to reusing the suitable terms in their data straight away and not worry about making the entire external ontologies available along with their data: the fact that terminologies are represented through dereferenceable URIs provides a mechanism to obtain the originating ontology by looking up one of its terms.

In this regard, the set of Web ontologies can be seen as a data lake itself: a pool from which the terms can be picked as necessary for the data schemas, without assuming responsibility for the entire ontologies because of it, hence the distinction between *ontologies* and *schemas*. The only implicit commitment is that the ontology engineer accepts the underlying model of the terms being reused. Consequently, the adoption of the reused terminologies is assumed to comply with the semantics indicated by the ontology, and therefore, that the data are not logically inconsistent according to it.

7.2.1. *Distributed data storage and querying with linked data graphs*

We have discussed how the organization of linked data into graphs provides a way to characterize datasets in an ecosystem that, theoretically, does not *require* to be partitioned into datasets and would, in fact, still work if they were not organized into datasets. Indeed, the entire ensemble of existing linked data on the Web may be regarded as a single, huge graph, if one that is not necessarily able to guarantee complete graph connectivity, upon which the construction of datasets as graphs is applied. By that philosophy, it matters little where one or more such constructed RDF graphs are stored. There is no implied mapping between SPARQL endpoints, RDF graphs and data stores.

By combining the flexibility of the SPARQL language, the standard nature of its HTTP service bindings and the principles of data and schema reuse, there appears a further characteristic of the Linked Data paradigm, which helps overcome the issue of not knowing the data being managed. Linked data sport a property that may be summarized as *self-queriability*: simply put, one can study the shape and schema of a linked dataset by issuing queries in the same language used for obtaining the actual data, and the same predicates in that language on top of that. Consider for example this simple SPARQL query:

```
SELECT DISTINCT ?domain ?op ?range
WHERE {
    [a ?domain] ?op [a ?range]
}
```

Essentially, this query enumerates the object properties op of all the data accessible through the SPARQL endpoint: they are object properties because the objects must have an RDF type (through the "a" shorthand for "rdf:type") as much as the subjects, therefore they cannot be literals. The query also lists the "top-down" domains and ranges for each property, i.e. the types of entities that have that property, and to those referenced by it *in those data*[8], as opposed to the asserted domain and range that define the properties themselves in an ontology.

Consider for instance Event Ontology[9], which can be used to describe events of any kind, from historical events to microscopic system events fired by a computer's operating system. Because it is generic, this ontology defines a event:agent property having range foaf:Agent, a class that can be specialized into anything from people to animals or can run instances of an application. If we run the SPARQL query above over an Internet of Things dataset, the results can tell us that the predicates using event:agent all point

---

8 It is considered a reasonable assumption here, that all RDF resources are given at least one explicit rdf:type.

9 Event Ontology: http://motools.sourceforge.net/event/.

to objects of the Sensor type from the aforementioned SSN ontology. One can then surmise that, in this dataset sensors are the only agents that participate in events, thus further delineating the Internet of Things nature of the data, even where this was not made explicit anywhere in the dataset metadata.

The above query is very useful for getting a rough idea of the shape of a dataset of which we know nothing: for this reason it is also called an *exploratory query*. It also proves that, unlike SQL-based silos, there is no need for specific verbs in the language to query a data store for its schema: in SPARQL, one can query a dataset for its schema as they would for its data. The user will still formulate the body of a query in terms of graph patterns (subject, predicate, object and possibly context); it is merely a matter of where to place variables in these graph patterns.

Several techniques exist for performing bottom-up analyses of linked datasets, aiming to produce what has been called the "emergent schema" or "emergent knowledge" [PHA 16, PRE 11]. Most of these techniques rely on prototypical or exploratory queries, i.e. standard SPARQL queries that are expected to be satisfied by any linked dataset. They can be used to bridge the structure of a dataset with its semantics, since they return information such as which classes are typically associated with which properties and which property sequences, or *chains*, are established in the data.

7.2.2. *Describing and profiling data sources*

Over the course of the Big Data age, it has become increasingly important to make it easy for a dataset to be discovered so that its content can be retrieved. The rise of open catalogs and dedicated search engines like *Kaggle*[10], *Data Hub*[11], *Google Dataset Search*[12] or *Zenodo*[13], coupled with the emergence of recommendations and guidelines such as the FAIR principles for research data[14], is tangible proof of how crucial it is to respond to this need nowadays. Guidelines like the FAIR principles entail a series of

---

10 Kaggle: https://www.kaggle.com/.

11 Data Hub: https://datahub.io/.

12 Google Dataset Search (beta): https://toolbox.google.com/datasetsearch.

13 Zenodo: https://zenodo.org/.

14 FAIR stands for Findable, Accessible, Interoperable and Reusable, see https://www.go-fair.org/fair-principles/.

implications that encompass technical, legal and operational aspects. Data cataloging can be seen as an enabler for the exploitation of data in a data lake, and a basic utility for a coarse organization of its content.

To facilitate its inclusion into a data catalog, and by extension make it more exploitable, a dataset needs either to describe itself, or to be easily described by an external agent: this is formally achieved through the provision of *metadata*, which, as discussed earlier in Chapter 4, are data that describe the nature, characteristics, permissions, history and provenance (or *lineage*) of other data. Metadata can be parsed and interpreted by catalogs, so that a catalog's entry for that dataset can be returned when an appropriate query is issued upon the catalog or search engine. But what are the metadata that typically characterize (or should characterize) a linked dataset? How easy is it to generate them out of the data themselves, and how important are those that cannot be generated in this way? Answering these questions will offer insight into how suitable the Linked Data paradigm is as a mechanism for making sense of data in a data lake.

There are several proposed standards that address the way a dataset made with Linked Data should be described. These mostly come in the form of metadata vocabularies, i.e. the terms to be used in the schemas of a "meta-dataset", and in some cases their scope extends to encompass non-linked datasets as well. The Vocabulary of Interlinked Datasets (VoID)[15] is a proposed metadata vocabulary for describing – structurally, operationally and with basic statistical and semantic information – RDF datasets as well as *linksets*, or datasets containing only RDF links between datasets. VoID integrates standard metadata from the Dublin Core vocabulary with a bespoke terminology indicating how the semantics of a dataset are organized in terms of the ontologies it uses in its schema, and how the data can be partitioned in terms of the usage of classes and properties from those ontologies. It also provides basic statistics (number of triples in the whole dataset and in its parts) as well as operational information, such as the regular expressions that can match the URIs of entities in the datasets, the locations of the downloadable data dumps and their formats, and where the Web service endpoint for SPARQL queries is expected to be available.

---

15 Vocabulary of Interlinked Datasets: https://www.w3.org/TR/void/.

Through the description of a linkset, VoID can be used to describe mappings in the data, from and to which datasets and using which properties for the mapping. Note that a significant part of the VoID description of a dataset can be reconstructed from the data itself. Class and property partitions, statistics in number of triples, vocabularies used and some references to other datasets can all be generated as a synthesis of the data itself. While the same does not hold for information such as the data dump or SPARQL endpoint locations, the usage of URIs and namespaces for the identification of datasets provides possible entry points to heuristics able to discover them automatically.

Another metadata vocabulary built in RDF specifically for cataloging is DCAT[16], a recommendation of the World Wide Web Consortium aimed at facilitating catalog interoperability. DCAT allows the construction of profiles by combining descriptions of the datasets themselves, their distributions, associated Web services and the catalogs that contain entries about them. A dataset profile in DCAT can be complemented with additional predicates from VoID, Dublin Core and other vocabularies. While VoID provides the fundamental elements of structural semantics (e.g. which classes and properties to use) for querying a dataset, DCAT allows for finer-grained semantics that can help the user in understanding how suitable a dataset is for the task at hand. It is possible to specify the spatial and temporal coverage of the content of a dataset, up to quantifying the minimum spatial and temporal distance between data units, and to thematically relate a dataset to an entire taxonomy or parts thereof.

As DCAT profiles contain information for the user that go beyond the technical underpinnings of dataset consumption, it is also much more difficult, where at all possible, to reconstruct this information from the actual data. Although semantically characterizing a dataset can be a daunting effort that may require the employment of classifiers, a dataset generated as Linked Data is capable of supporting the process. For one thing, if a dataset reuses standard domain-specific ontologies in its schema, this already restricts the possible topics addressed by it, as they are often embedded in the ontology domains. For example, if a dataset makes extensive usage of the

---

16 Data Catalog Vocabulary, version 2: https://www.w3.org/TR/vocab-dcat-2/.

`AirPollutantSensor` class from the M3-lite ontology[17], then it can be inferred that the dataset collects sensor data – although this tells us nothing about where and when these sensors have been collecting their data. If, on the other hand, the dataset also references geographical locations from other datasets such as GeoNames[18], possibly by being paired to a linkset, then it is possible to take advantage of the linking to lift existing information, such as the country or region of a city and the coordinates of a location, so as to approximate the spatial coverage of the dataset.

To summarize, the interplay between the Linked Data principles and the adoption of metadata vocabularies following the same principles provides a way for a dataset to be given a definite identity within a data lake. In this way, the data can be directly exploited, both technically and semantically, in the format (RDF) in which they were originally created and stored. This is best achieved if the potential offered by the underlying representation is properly exploited at data generation time, by performing as much interlinking as possible with widely adopted datasets and reusing the most suitable known ontologies as part of the dataset schema.

7.2.3. *Integrating internal and external data*

We have said that there is no implied association between SPARQL endpoints, RDF graphs and data stores. Indeed, Linked Data standards mandate that it should be possible to access any RDF graph exposed by any SPARQL endpoint from any location: in fact, a single service endpoint can be used to access many graphs from multiple RDF stores at once.

This distributed access takes place either without the user's knowledge of who is formulating the query, to answer which *data integration* process takes place in the background, or it is explicitly stated by the user as part of a federated query, whereupon a *data federation* process occurs. In the latter case, the user designates a node (here represented by a SPARQL service endpoint) and delegates to that node the responsibility to fetch from the other indicated nodes the data that will ultimately answer their query.

---

17 A multimedia ontology specialized for sensing devices: http://purl.org/iot/vocab/m3-lite#AirPollutantSensor.

18 GeoNames: https://www.geonames.org/.

In terms of Linked Data standards, linkage by means of giving every describable thing a URI provides a basic mechanism for data integration, which is valid for any dataset regardless of the schema used. There are at least two ways of integrating data from other RDF datasets using this standard mechanism:

1) Dereferencing the URIs of an entity being reused, which is made possible by adhering to the second basic principle (identifiers that can be looked up), and by the third one (standardized representation language), which delivers data that describe that entity in RDF format. This means those data can be imported there and then to enrich whatever description is published for that entity by the originating dataset.

2) Federated SPARQL queries, which are able to process data fetched directly from other external sources that are explicitly indicated in the query itself.

As for the latter method, the W3C provides a specification for formulating federated queries [BUI 13] using a SERVICE clause that encompasses all and only the triple patterns for which we want results to be returned by that query service.

If, for instance, we have a dataset about musical performances, we may want to know how many times a national anthem was performed in each country. However, since the dataset is not a geographical one, it might not always have information of which country each city is located in, or whether a certain location is a country or not. If the locations used in the dataset have been reused from another dataset, for example DBpedia, then we can ask DBpedia itself for the countries, like so[19]:

```
SELECT ?country (COUNT(DISTINCT ?performance) as
                ?performances)
WHERE {
    # The performances happened somewhere: could be a
    # country, region, city or a place within a city
    ?performance event:place ?place ;
```

```
# They  must  be  national  anthems
mo: genre  < http :// dbpedia . org / resource / National_anthem >

# Ask  DBpedia  in  which  country  each  place  is ...
SERVICE  SILENT  < http :// dbpedia . org / sparql > {
    {  ?place  dbpo: country  ?country  }
    #  ... unless  the  place  itself  is  a  country
    UNION  {  ?place  a  dbpo: Country  BIND(?place  as
                    ?country )  }
}
} GROUP  BY  ?country
```

Data integration in federated queries is straightforward, since the terms of the integration are declared in the query syntax through using the same variables (i.e. place in the case above) to specify bindings across triple patterns. Federated SPARQL queries are exact, meaning that the query processing engines of the services involved will typically only return the results that exactly match the provided triple patterns, without performing approximations or taking ontology alignments into account. Therefore, for the above integration mechanism to work, it is assumed that the user knows the representation schemas adopted by each member of the integration: in data lakes, this is not a given, however in Linked Data these schemas can be easily discovered, to an extent, by means of exploratory queries.

The downside of this approach is that, with the rules for integration being hard-coded in the query for retrieving the data, the burden of managing these rules still falls on the final consumer of the data, despite it being fairly easy to generate rules that approximate precise data integration. There are also software systems that, given a canonical non-federated SPARQL query, attempt to fetch results from multiple datasets that are able to satisfy at least some part of the query. This is generally not transparent, meaning that the user does not need to specify, or does not even need to be aware of, which datasets to query for which patterns in the original query.

In the literature, the line that divides data integration from data federation is rather blurred. The approach taken by the definition of SPARQL federated queries is that a federation can, in principle, be repeated on any endpoint in the Linked Data cloud, with only minor adjustments in the SERVICE clauses, as each node used to bootstrap the process delivers the same results as any other

[SHE 90]. Other schools of thought use either term alternatively. In this book, the distinction is made explicit in order to highlight how it relates to data lakes.

From a Linked Data perspective, federation requires not only knowledge of the dataset schemas (which, as we have seen, can be discovered bottom-up to some extent), but also very precise knowledge of how these datasets, each with its own schema, are distributed across SPARQL endpoints and possibly even RDF graphs. This configures a landscape of data that, tied as it is to Web service endpoints and dataset partitioning, hardly resembles a lake. Pure source-agnostic data integration which, as we have seen, is non-normative in Linked Data but still possible, more closely resembles how one would expect a consumer to interact with data lakes, i.e. by issuing a query that conforms to a single – possibly expanded – schema, ignoring which data sources will satisfy which parts of the schema.

7.3. Limitations and issues

By choosing to generate a novel set of data by the Linked Data principles, it is possible to create and publish a resource that can, to a large extent, be understood "as-is" and interpreted without having to consult the knowledge engineers who created it. All it takes is a judicious choice of terms and awareness of interconnected external data. Possible ways of implementing these principles include choosing RDF as a storage and publishing format, using known ontologies as the source of terms for the data schema and referencing external data URIs. The resulting dataset will have characteristics that are highly desirable in the context of a data lake, as making sense of it by directly inspecting the data can be made significantly easier. Not every challenge posed by data lakes, however, can be addressed with such ease through Linked Data alone, and the knowledge engineer responsible for creating a dataset can only go so far in ensuring the exploitability of its content in the far future.

Linked Data is about standards, be they formal, such as W3C recommendations, ISO or IEEE standards, or *de facto*, i.e. perceived through widespread adoption and shared understanding. This implies that the exploitability of a dataset depends on the health of the ecosystem in which it was born, such as the Linked Open Data Cloud[20] and the network of Web ontologies. Many commonly used ontologies for a given domain may not have reached a formal standard status, but still enjoy wide adoption due to being the highest-quality, the most widely disseminated or the only available RDF vocabularies in existence for a given domain. In such cases, the maintenance of the ontologies (for example, the online availability of the RDF documents that represent them) and of their documentation is a responsibility of their creators, and the stability and constant availability of these resources could change unpredictably. The documentation of an ontology could even be taken offline after a few years, not picked up by archival services such as the Internet Archive and subsequently be lost forever. Still, the corresponding ontology would still live in the form of its usage within datasets, but it would be more difficult to interpret the corresponding data, especially if the terminology is ambiguous unless resolved by parsing the actual ontology or studying its specification. This has the effect of making the semantics of data latent, in that their meaning is driven by undocumented ontologies.

A similar argument can be posed for external data that are referenced by the dataset: if these are lost or significantly altered without there being a clear reference to a specific version of the dataset at the time it was linked to, then the ability to integrate external knowledge may be negatively affected. This leads to another issue that is often found in data lakes and which Linked Data principles are not designed to address, which is the historical perspective on the data. Typically, when consuming data from a SPARQL query service, or by resolving the URI of an entity online, the output we will be looking at will most likely be a snapshot, i.e. the set of facts that are true for that entity at the time we are scrutinizing it. For example, suppose a university publishes a linked dataset of the research profiles of its employees. As researchers join or leave the university, the published data will likely only cover the researchers employed there at that time, and there is no guarantee that the data of former employees will be available the way they were when said researchers were working in that university. Likewise, the data could indicate only the current director of a department and not the history of its directors. From the perspective of a data lake, when looking at the raw RDF it can be hard to assess during what period the stated facts held true.

---

20 The Linked Open Data Cloud: https://lod-cloud.net/.

The one described above is a greater issue than a mere question of personal privacy of former employees: it is also a potential design issue caused by the "simplicity trap" of the RDF paradigm. Because the organization of data into triples is so simple, one may be tricked into believing it is only useful for encoding simple facts between two named entities, for instance *<John, directorOf, ComputerScienceDepartment>*, without a real possibility to contextualize the truthfulness of such a fact. The DBpedia dataset is a notable example of this fallacy, which is actually inherited from the structure of Wikipedia pages. In practice, contextual information representation can by all means be achieved using Linked Data. The solutions can be implemented:

1) in the management of the entire datasets, for example by providing a versioning or history tracking system;

2) in the data model itself, for example through the *reification* of facts, which is the generation of entities that embody the validity of the statements themselves.

In a data lake context, where all we can assume to have is the raw dataset, a solution of the second category is preferable, as the availability of a support system for version tracking cannot be assumed over time. Also, while some proposed mechanisms for tracking data versions are being evaluated by the research community, none have, as of yet, been standardized. To deal with the above examples by enhancing the data model, one could reify the memberships and roles of employees and directors by creating bespoke entities for them, each with its own URI and types and different from the entity that represents the employee as a person. As a demonstration of the benefits of ontology reuse, there is a W3C standard vocabulary for dealing with exactly this problem[21]. Once we have an *ad hoc* entity for a membership, we can attach to it whatever peripheral information may help restricting its validity, such as the start/end dates of the job, the role specification, the person and the department. Standard vocabularies exist for reifying other recurrent types of data such as processes and events, be they macroscopic (e.g. history) or microscopic (e.g. system logs).

---

21 See the `Membership` class of the W3C Organization ontology: https://www.w3.org/TR/vocab-org/.

The issues described in this section are not to be intended as problems raised by the Linked Data paradigm per se: rather, they are issues that it was not explicitly developed to solve. The big contribution of Linked Data to data lakes is to help preserve the interpretability of data over time. Whereas the quality of data links ultimately depends on the health of the overarching ecosystem, other issues, such as tracking provenance and preserving the validity of facts, can be tackled by making accurate design choices at the time of generating the data. Using reification does come with a cost in terms of the size of the dataset and the need to explore more than just the "immediate surroundings" of an entity to understand it, which raises potential performance concerns. However, the approach pays off in exactly the way a data lake ecosystem requires: by keeping the data valid and understandable regardless of when they will be used. So too, many of these design choices can be made irrespective of the foreseen future usage of the data, which is again inline with one of the key postulates of data lakes.

7.4. The smart cities use case

Some data-driven or data-intensive application domains, owing to their (usually intentional) generality, do not come with clear established data requirements and workflows from the start. There are usually a few use cases that warrant the start of a new project in these domains, but ulterior goals and further use cases may emerge once it becomes clearer what data can be concretely obtained – for example due to the project being adopted.

Largely unexplored fields of research are naturally subjected to this issue, as they presuppose openness to emerging and serendipitous research problems. Open application domains on a large scale are also affected, as it cannot always be predicted which kinds of data will remain and become useful for which use cases. Smart cities are an example of one such application domain, being so vast and susceptible to changes in their use cases alongside the needs and habits of citizens.

Researchers in smart cities study the potential for the incorporation of information technologies to improve the quality and societal impact of urban services, while containing the cost, overhead and environmental impact of doing so. When a city embarks on a journey towards becoming a smart city, it will typically do so on the basis of a small set of use cases that pertain to that city, such as delivering real-time updates on public transport or optimizing the power consumption of streetlights. However, more previously unthought-of use cases may later become relevant for that city.

From a data perspective, the set of urban data to be acquired could partly be known *a priori*, and could partly be acquired as the interest around the project increases. It is generally a success factor for a smart city project to be able to source further types of data from new providers, and to quickly establish operational pipelines for acquiring them, even when the use cases that these data can service are not yet delineated. This, however, implies that urban data may need to be acquired before knowing how they will be used, and therefore that the schema to represent these data must be flexible enough to facilitate their future adoption in unpredicted use cases, yet clear enough for those data to be made sense of at that time. Concurrently, the amounts of data generated, for example by sensors scattered around the city, can be huge. This combination of vast amounts of data and a partial view on when and how they will be used constitutes the typical scenario of a data lake.

In what follows, an example will be provided on how a smart city infrastructure uses Linked Data to address issues typically associated with data lakes.

7.4.1. *The MK Data Hub*

Among the cities that undertook endeavours to improve the quality of their services, the case of Milton Keynes in the UK is emblematic for its focus on the way its open data are managed. These efforts took the form of a series of funded projects and initiatives throughout the 2010s, with MK:Smart[22] first and then cityLABS[23], both notable for being particularly data-driven and focused on the Internet of Things. With only an initial set of use cases being addressed, these projects adopted a policy of gathering as many data from as many sources as possible, and providing means to facilitate their consumption by third parties. This in turn has led to the expansion of the serviceable use cases, which encompass public transport, smart parking, energy and water consumption as well as citizen engagement and enterprise development.

---

22 MK:Smart: https://www.mksmart.org/.
23 cityLABS: https://www.citylabs.org.uk/.

The technological stack that supports Milton Keynes in the adoption of data-driven technologies constitutes a distributed infrastructure of services that are diversified in the domains, formats and timeliness of the data that they deliver. Data sources are a decentralized set of Web services, delivered as HTTP APIs[24] exposed through several service endpoints on the Web. All the datasets and service endpoints are however cataloged by a single online portal: the MK Data Hub[25]. This Web-based facility provides exploratory functionalities as well as unified access to the data. The datasets registered with the MK Data Hub are open, though some of them may require a free subscription in order to generate access credentials.

The services registered with the MK Data Hub publish data of one or two broad categories:

– streams of data updated in real-time;

– data that are either "static", i.e. offered one-off by a specific provider and not requiring updates, or updated over a long period like monthly or yearly.

Examples of streamed data include weather station reports, live public transport routes and available spaces in public car parks. They are typically stored in continuously updated relational databases and published as XML or JSON data streams, depending on the client request. Streams are usually limited in the temporal window or the number of data points provided. Non-streamed data include the locations of charging stations for electric vehicles, bus stops or quality-of-life statistics on the various areas of the city, such as housing prices, crime and census. These data are published in various formats depending on the provider, ranging from simple downloadable data dumps in comma-separated values (CSV) to RDF data that can be queried through SPARQL endpoints. SPARQL query answers, in turn, can be serialized in one of many formats, including several formats based on XML and JSON and, depending on the verb of the query, also CSV or native RDF formats like N-Triples[26] and Turtle[27].

---

24 Application programming interfaces running on top of the standard HyperText Transfer Protocol of the World Wide Web.

25 MK Data Hub: https://datahub.mksmart.org.

26 See: https://www.w3.org/2001/sw/RDFCore/ntriples/.

27 See: https://www.w3.org/TR/turtle/.

Unlike streamed data, "static" data are not stored using a different schema than the one used for publishing them: they exist in their original raw form to accommodate use cases that require their integration or transformation. When looking at this aspect of Milton Keynes' urban open data, we are therefore in the presence of a data lake.

7.4.2. *Linked data in the MK Data Hub*

In an infrastructure such as that of data lakes, which is relatively flat in terms of abstraction from storage, the primary way of consuming the data is by fetching and inspecting a dataset as a whole. The catalog portion of the MK Data Hub[28] provides a view that reflects this partitioning, by listing datasets and providing a way to access each one independently. Among the listed datasets, for instance, there is one of gas consumption statistics by area (LSOA), several crime statistics (one dataset per type of crime) and several census datasets, each of them covering all the areas of Milton Keynes over a particular dimension such as population, occupation, marital status and disabilities.

However, this is not necessarily the only way, or even the preferred way, for a client application to query the data that satisfy its own use case. For example, a service that offers insights to citizens as to which area of the city they should relocate[29] needs to be able to answer a user query of the type *"Tell me everything you know about a specific area of Milton Keynes that is related to quality of life."* A data lake organized only by dataset's would be very inefficient at answering such a query straight away, as it would have to inspect every candidate dataset for anything that may pertain to the area being considered. Indices may be built on top of these datasets for efficient retrieval, but even so it can be very difficult to determine how to index a dataset *semantically*, in a meaningful way for users and applications.

The Milton Keynes smart city data infrastructure preserves this data lake substrate, but avails itself of the Linked Data principles to provide alternative ways to consume its data when the need for doing so arises. The workflow that manages the registration of a dataset includes the following three steps:

---

28 MK Data Hub catalog: https://datahub.mksmart.org/data-catalogue/.

29 One such application is provided by the MK:Smart project itself at https://datahub.mksmart.org/demos/eduvocation/.

– convert the data provided to RDF and store them as such, exposing each for querying via SPARQL endpoints;

– build a semantic profile (also in RDF) for each dataset, including those already made available in RDF by third parties, and register it with the data catalog;

– integrate the dataset profile with mappings and rewriting rules to automatically identify entities in that dataset and extract the data relevant for that entity.

Each step is tied to one of the three use cases for Linked Data usage in data lakes, which were illustrated in section 7.2.

Distributed storage and querying: statistics, such as crime or deprivation indices, are typically made available by various bodies of the city council at different intervals. They are typically organized into statistical observations, e.g. one per spreadsheet or CSV file, and each observation is a list of rows, e.g. one per administrative area of the city. The conversion to RDF reorganizes the data so that they can be queries more efficiently, but ultimately preserves their semantics as statistical observations: at this stage, there is no attempt to identify entities that may be of interest to users or applications.

Consider for instance the following snippet of data (in Turtle format):

```
@prefix  arw:  <http://data.mksmart.org/tmpns/mkc/Fire/Arson−Wards/
        row/>  .
@prefix  stat:  <http://vocab.sindice.net/csv/>  .
@prefix  xsd:  <http://www.w3.org/2001/XMLSchema#>  .

<http://data.mksmart.org/tmpns/mkc/Fire/Arson−Wards/>
   a  <http://purl.org/linked−data/cube#Observation>
   ;  stat:numberOfRows  "288"^^xsd:integer
   ;  stat:numberOfColumns  "3"^^xsd:integer
   ;  stat:row  <http://data.mksmart.org/tmpns/mkc/Fire/Arson−Wards/
        row/0>
   #  , rows 1, 2...

<http://data.mksmart.org/tmpns/mkc/Fire/Arson−Wards/row/0>
   a  stat:Row
   ;  stat:rowPosition  "0"
   ;  arw:numberOfArsonFires  "1389"^^xsd:integer
   ;  arw:Year  "2001/2"^^xsd:string
   ;  arw:Geography  "MK6"^^xsd:string
```

It describes a statistical observation named with the URI <http://data. mksmart.org/tmpns/mkc/Fire/Arson-Wards/>, which has 288 rows and one of them (row 0) says that there were 1389 arson fires during the period called "2001/2" in the area with code MK6. Note that the properties of a row are defined in the namespace of this observation dataset alone – here abbreviated with the prefix arw – as there are no alignments with other observation datasets yet, not even those about other types of crime. However, the RDF terms of statistical data prefixe with stat, being taken from a shared ontology, allow for a quick understanding of the nature of this dataset.

Every dataset offered by the data provider is assigned its own RDF graph in order to preserve its identity as a dataset, however this is without detriment to the ability to query multiple graphs together, since: (i) a single SPARQL endpoint is able to seamlessly merge results from multiple graphs stored together, and (ii) graphs stored behind different SPARQL endpoints can still be queried in a federated way, as illustrated in section 7.2.1.

Dataset profiling: each dataset is paired with an RDF description whose schema combines VoID, DCAT (see section 7.2.2) and a custom vocabulary. One such dataset profile will contain the name of the RDF graph associated with the dataset, the SPARQL endpoint to access it, the classes and properties used – in this case mostly related to statistical observations – and indications of the spatial and temporal coverage extracted, for example, from the properties arw:Year and arw:Geography in the above data.

Data integration: this is where the organization of datasets and the knowledge extracted from them come together to generate a high-level representation of a query response out of a data lake. The goal can be, for example, to obtain integrated quality-of-life information for the area identified as MK6: to that end, specific properties of statistical observations should disappear, as should the order and numbering of rows, as they are most likely irrelevant to the end consumer of the data.

After the dataset profile has been generated, a set of mappings and rewrite rules is paired with it. The purpose of these rules is manifold:

– to specify the types of high-level entities, such as areas, postcodes, years and quality-of-life parameters, which the dataset can contribute to;

– to indicate how to locate the entities themselves, for example that the system should take the value of arw:Geography to identify a postcode in this dataset, as in another dataset it may identify another type of geographical area;

– to specify how the associated data should be transformed in the integrated view.

These rules are expressed in various forms, including regular expressions (for rules of the second type) and lightweight functions written in the JavaScript programming language. Their output is then injected into SPARQL query templates that are part of the integration logic, to generate the final SPARQL query that will retrieve data for a given entity of a given type on that particular dataset.

By executing these integration rules, each one applied to its corresponding dataset, it is possible to query multiple datasets at the same time and generate a holistic view of the administrative area identified by postcode MK6. An example is provided by the following snippet in a custom JSON format:

```
{
    "type"      : "administrative_area",
    "postcode": "MK6",
    "name"      : "Tinkers Bridge",
    "stats"    : {
        "arsons" : [{
            "period" : {
                "start" : 2001,
                "end"    : 2002
            },
            "amount" : 1389
        },{
          # ... other periods ...
        }],
        # ... other data ...
    }
}
```

The same or similar rules may however be applied to generate data in any other format of choice.

By implementing such a workflow using Linked Data principles and technologies, it is therefore possible to capture and store large amounts of data relatively quickly, as the initial extraction phase applies just the necessary amount of semantics to the schema in order to gain an understanding of the nature of the data. The adoption of standards such as RDF and SPARQL offer lasting advantages, such as the ability to store the data anywhere and high flexibility in designing their schema. By combining shared ontologies and dataset profiles, it is then possible to implement further layers, here exemplified by the integration rules, to generate high-level representations of the content of a data lake.

7.5. Take-home message

Linked Data is more of a paradigm than a set of technologies, whose principles have the potential to hold across generations even as its reference technology stack evolves, or even in contexts where other technologies than the reference ones are adopted. These principles are a natural fit for the context of data lakes, insofar as the problems they tackle are related to future interpretations of the data therein. The pivotal element of these principles is a shared representation not only in terms of standard formats, but also in terms of shareable conceptualizations of the data domains, which take the form of terms, ontologies, as well as references to other data. There is still much work ahead for researchers in this field, especially when it comes to dealing with the evolution and sustainability of data, as well as the performance of their consumption. While it is not meant as a panacea to all the computational problems that data analytics face today, Linked Data presents opportunities for addressing semantic aspects in the early phases of the generation of a dataset, thus keeping a data lake meaningful and exploitable for as long as the ecosystem of ontologies behind it stays reasonably healthy.

Fog Computing

8.1. Introduction

In the data lake concept, all data are ingested, no matter their volume, their variety and their velocity. Storing all these data could be a challenge even if technology offers several solutions in terms of infrastructure and environment such as on premise, on cloud or hybrid cloud. The Internet of Things (IoT) has changed the concept of data acquisition into the data lake environment, and for some data lakes, volume limits could be reached in the near future. An interesting concept, named *fog computing*, has been recently introduced. One main characteristic of fog computing is the sharing of data ingestion steps between the sensors which produce data, and the data lake which consumes data.

This chapter first explains the concept of fog computing and the associated challenges and then discusses the different options to be taken into account when dealing with a data lake.

8.2. A little bit of context

The cloud is often seen by the end user as an infinite space, where all of their data could be stored, accessed, shared and curated easily. That was indeed the case when the Internet was mainly there to store data produced by humans. Its main features were to store and share data like videos, songs,

---

Chapter written by Arnault IOUALALEN.

texts and hypertexts. However, this is changing gradually since numerous objects now also consume bandwidth and cloud storage to manipulate the data they produce. The key change concerns who (or what) is using these data and what for. Traditionally, the market value of data comes from the human analysis of a lot of data produced by a machine.

For example, a chart aggregates data which in return create value for a decision process of a person. However, this requires us to have a model, in advance, in order to store the data in a relevant way and to produce meaningful information. The problem is that with the growing number of connected objects, the sources of data are now increasingly diverse and less structured. It becomes more difficult to know, from a human perspective, if there is value or not in the ocean of swirling data, and it is even more difficult to extract information from it.

Consequently, it is now up to machines to interact between themselves to create value all along the streams of data. The traditional idea that data is produced by machines and consumed by humans now includes new machine intermediaries that are both producers and consumers. Hence, it is said that the Internet of humans has gradually shifted toward an Internet of Things.

8.3. Every machine talks

Before the Internet of Things touched the public, it has incubated inside factories for many years now. Because competition between companies has intensified, traditional industries have been forced to drive their costs down. Companies needed to find new ways to cut both internal and external costs, and automation has played a major role in slashing internal costs. The main idea was to do a one-time major investment (backed by bankers or investors) to boost productivity by modernizing their production process.

It started with human-operated machines, then semi-automated machinery and now almost fully automated factories. These investments are only profitable though if they are efficiently controlled. Machines could break, like humans can become ill. In order to find a good trade-off between manpower and machines, many factories now embed thousands of sensors in order to inform the few operators left if everything is working perfectly or not. This means that a production tool started to look like a black box that communicates a lot about itself to allow another operator to monitor its health. Following that logic, more and more layers of automation piled one on top of another. Each layer reported to, a higher one that in return, curated the information and passed on new information to the following layer.

However, it is not only automation that made machines talk. The use of sensors has been designed to replace humans performing many menial and tedious tasks of inspection. For example, gradually every container in every ship has been given a sensor for detecting whether it has been breached, whether it is too hot or too cold or whether a fire has occurred.

The current industrial age is turning every object into something that communicates, that informs whomever or whatever needs to know something about it or around it. And the Internet is its vector, as every message sent uses the classical network stack of protocols to be transmitted (usually after passing through some local gateway). However, there is not necessarily some receiver for any given message, so the cloud serves as a buffer to hold the message, hoping that it would be used, passed on or transformed by some other process later.

This introduces two main issues. First, the space available to store these data on the cloud is challenged more and more every day. Second, all of these communications create a flood of information from which it is complicated to extract any meaningful knowledge. The challenge is then to find a way to construct knowledge from an ever-increasing volume of unstructured data. And for any new challenge, there is a way to monetize it. All of the Internet giants know this and hence invest massively in the Internet infrastructure, in order to allow data to be generated and monetized.

8.4. The volume paradox

A few years ago, Moore's law, which states that the computing power of computers doubles every year, started to be contested. The computing power achievable through integrated circuits started to hit the physical limit of miniaturization. The growth would then only be achieved by parallelizing the computational power instead of locally increasing it.

This allowed multi-threading technology, multi-core and then grid computing. As the computational power of each single device would not grow, the overall accessible power will grow by adding more and more devices, capable of computing and viewing them as a single one. This is like a few decades ago, when the SETI program was one of the first attempts to tap into the dispersed computational power of idling computers through the Internet.

The Internet of Things is viewed as an opportunity to decentralize computational power even more, as the number of devices is growing rapidly. For example, in 2015, there were 15 billion devices with computational capability. However, 85% of them were not connected to the Internet. Analysts suggest that by 2020, there will be 50 billion connected objects, which means that the computational power available could follow Moore's law again.

The risk is that the volume of data to handle will surpass either the overall computational capabilities or the bandwidth (or both). One thing is certain, the current architecture of the cloud will not handle this growth by itself. This is the current paradox of the Internet of Things that is emerging: the more decentralized it gets, the stronger both of its connections and connecting node have to be to withhold it. As the stream of data grows in an uncontrollable way, a shift is taking place to avoid this paradox.

8.5. The fog, a shift in paradigm

The main origin of the volume paradox comes from the fact that every communicating object is speaking freely and directly to potentially the whole network. The network itself is seen as an unstructured form able to store and digest everything thrown at it.

One way to avoid this is to improve the quality of the information passing through it before hand. By doing so, the network has to handle fewer messages but with more knowledge within, instead of a flood of messages filled with raw data. In order to do this, it is necessary to bring closer to the data producer, the intelligence capable of curating it and extracting knowledge from it. This is the basis for fog computing.

On this paradigm, the stream of data would be first aggregated by some local entity, which could be some specific device (a router, for example), some ad hoc network (through a certain protocol) or a node, on the road toward the cloud. However, nothing prevents the architect from designing new layers upon it and creating a full stack of communication protocols between all curating nodes.

For example, let us look at an industrial usage of this paradigm with modern cars. Nowadays, cars are equipped with many radars and cameras. In order to improve driving, cars send a lot of information to the car manufacturers. For example, they can send engine status, temperature, radar data, images and so on. With all of these data producers, it is possible to have a real-time stream of information about the condition of the cars and their environment. These data could be highly valuable if treated properly.

One way to look at it is to build a giant network connecting all the cars to some database, and design some system for digging in it. The problem is that the bandwidth and the storage capability will have trouble scaling to the volume of data to process. Another way is to equip the cars with computational capability in order to make them send only relevant information instead of a stream of raw data. In doing so, the car would be a fog in itself as it curates its own data before sending it. Even then, there will still be a lot of information centralized for nothing.

For example, if a car detects some icy road ahead, it will decide to notify it and send a message. However, this message has no value for almost every car on earth except those cars that are currently nearby. And all the cars going through this road will send the exact same message as they all see the same ice on the same road. These messages should not all be stored and made accessible for everyone; a second layer would only keep these data for the time they are relevant (while the road is still icy) before either discarding them or saving them for further use. Indeed, this layer could send a message at some point to let know that this road is usually icy in winter from 4 am to 11 am. This information is highly valuable for a larger layer that encompasses all roads of the region and could have a use for local services for dispatching utility vehicles. Alternatively, it could be made publicly available for any GPS device.

To properly handle this information, three layers have been used, each one passing only highly curated knowledge: the car sends contextual information from raw sensor data, the local fog aggregates this information for only the users on the road that could be impacted by it; the last layer is able to obtain broader knowledge and improves the safety of all users. The same result in one centralized database would require storing a vast amount of data and would soon be too large to work in practice at a reasonable cost.

The key feature in this example is preventing data from flowing, freely into the network by having a stack of local devices able to decide what to do with the information, rather than just passing it on.

To summarize, this shift in paradigm comes from a complete change on how the data are processed by the user. When using a cloud first, the user transmits, then stores the data, before finally curating it. Under the fog paradigm, the process is to store first, then curate and finally transmit.

8.6. Constraint environment challenges

To build coherent data from a multitude of heterogeneous data producers, it is important to add some intermediate layers in the network where these data are exchanged.

However, this type of architecture poses new challenges that were conveniently avoided under the cloud paradigm; mainly, the cost of curating, transmitting and storing all the data were ignored. In the current Internet of Things paradigm, the industry will fight for reducing both the cost of production and the energy consumption.

The former will be important to deploy quickly on new markets with a business model of "hardware as a service", where adding any new sensors on a network would be cheap and effortless. The latter is crucial for the durability of every system. Currently, the industry is working on both embedded energy production and hardware energy consumption. The objective is clearly to gain durability by producing the energy needed locally and also reduce the energy footprint of the hardware.

This comes with new ways to store and process data and avoids the traditional ways of transmitting it, such as WiFi, Bluetooth or mobile network. This also requires the addition of small memory capability around the sensors and small chip, in order to process data on the fly. Concerning the embedded chip, the engineering issue is often between having a small dedicated circuit which will be energy-efficient but expensive to make (as it is custom made for a niche market) and having a more general purpose, off-the-self processor which will be cheaper, but with a higher energy footprint.

Interestingly, these challenges are a general concern in the embedded software industry, where hardware constraints are ubiquitous. From the satellite embedding hardware which is 20 years old in order to resist radiation, to the smart oil drill that has to resist the constant impact of g-force, these industries have to deal with highly constraint environments and strong durability objectives. To succeed, they have to combine the know-how of software engineers, hardware designers and network architects.

Given the variety of uses that the fog will create, the use of custom-designed systems will be favored at least at the beginning, to sustain the growth of the industry. However, this choice will impact the computing capability of every system on several levels.

The system engineers will have to choose from the capabilities available, such as integer, floating-point (with full IEEE754 compliance or not) or fixed-point arithmetic, and also whether it will run on 32- or 64-bit instructions or with custom-made precision. All of these choices will have an impact on the efficiency of the system and its durability. However, it will also have an impact on its numerical stability and the quality of data it will produce. Ultimately, it is confidence in the overall system that is impacted.

8.7. Calculations and local drift

Dispatching operations on an unstructured network with highly constrained computation capabilities poses several issues regarding accuracy and numerical stability, from both the hardware and network perspectives.

The risk is not only theoretical, since numerical instabilities have already caused catastrophes in the past. They were then mitigated by improving precision and having a clear data flow on how the computations operate. In the context of the fog, both of these solutions are not going to be available, which could lead to a resurgence of these issues, at a more global scale instead of just on one isolated system.

8.7.1. *A short memo about computer arithmetic*

For anyone with very little background about computer arithmetic and numerical computations, the first thing to understand is that infinity does not mix well with computers. As they have a finite amount of memory, processing power and time to run computation, computers cannot handle the infinite amount of numbers a human can think of.

Also numbers with an infinite number of digits, like π or $\frac{1}{3}$, would not be represented accurately as their decimal part will be rounded (or truncated) at some point. There are also numbers that at first glance seem easy to represent but are not, like $\frac{1}{10}$. In that case, it is because such numbers cannot be represented accurately in the binary format, whereas it is possible in the decimal format.

Floating-point arithmetic is the most commonly used arithmetic to represent decimal numbers on computers. A floating-point number is similar to a scientific notation (like in calculators). It is composed of a sign, a mantissa holding the decimal part of the number and an exponent. The IEEE754 standard gives the acceptable sizes of mantissa and exponent, as well as some special values (like infinity of Not A Number values). The standard usually comes on every processor with two flavors 32-bit (single precision) or 64-bit (double precision), but recent additions of the standard now allow 16-bit or 128-bit floating-point numbers.

Contrary to the usual belief, this arithmetic is not like real numbers. Due to rounding-error issues, most numbers are not represented accurately, and additionally, some basic rules of arithmetic do not hold. For example, using associativity, distributivity or factorization to transform a given mathematical formula can result in a new formula, the result of which is *different* from the result of the original one. This is especially problematic in many algorithms performing a large number of summations, since the order in which to do these sums will have an impact on the final result.

It is also worth pointing out two major sources of rounding errors that could cause a drift in numerical computations:

– the first is the absorption issue where, when adding a small value to a large one, the result could only represent the large one. This means that some

$a + b$ operations could lead to b even when $a \neq 0$ (which breaks the rule of unicity of neutral element used to define the very basic group in mathematics);

– the second is called catastrophic cancelation, which represents the loss of every significant (and correct) digit of the result due to a subtraction. This error occurs when two noisy values that are very close to one another are subtracted, leaving out at the end, only the noise they bear. The problem in that case is that it introduces a value into the calculation that is entirely made of non-significant digits.

8.7.2. *Instability from within*

When performing numerical operations, the precision used to physically run the computation is obviously an important aspect. However, the choice of the arithmetic used could also be as important. The Vancouver stock exchange bug is an interesting story to illustrate this point.

In 1982, the Vancouver stock exchange decided to use a new index to represent the performance of its industry. Originally set at the value 1000.000, it operated with an arithmetic where there were only three digits to store the decimal part. After only 22 months, the index value plummeted to a record low of 520. The reason was not an industry collapse – the market of Vancouver was doing well during the period - but the arithmetic used by the computer in charge of updating the index. Indeed, at the end of each update operation, it truncated the last decimal of the result instead of rounding it to the nearest number. By doing so, the index was systematically rounding down. However, by choosing a better way to perform the rounding, the index value would have been closer to actual value, i.e. 1098.892.

When the arithmetic was chosen to perform the computation, the difference between rounding and truncating was probably seen as negligible. However, the accumulation in time of the small representation errors due to arithmetic, could gradually lead to a big drift in the computation. From a purely computational perspective, the system was operating completely normally without having any critical fault or having raised any exception. The numerical flaw was by design and was not a bug that could bring the system to a halt and automatically raise an alarm. The only way to detect that there was a flaw in the system was by a human deciding that this index was failing at mimicking the actual state of the market. However, if no human was observing and suspecting the system, this bug could have been totally silent and would have run forever.

It is thus clear that special care should be given to any decision about hardware and precision as it can lead to silent bugs in a system, such as this. The main risk is that these decisions operate on a layer of the network where no human is observing the system and where there are only machine-to-machine transactions. As the system is drifting in its calculation, so are all subsequent operations conducted by the system. The end user, which is usually a person, would have a suspicion about the result produced by the system only at the very end, when this one has been completely derailing and is obviously misbehaving.

8.7.3. *Non-determinism from outside*

The accuracy of numerical computations is strongly dependent on both the precision used (32- or 64-bits) and the way these computations are performed. For example, when performing a summation, the accuracy of the output could significantly diverge between an evaluation performed as a binary tree and a fully sequential chain of summation. As another example, performing $(a+b)+(c+d)$ may not be the same as doing $((a+b)+c)+d$ or $a+(b+(c+d))$.

The reasons concern absorption and cancellation issues, as well as the fact that sums are no longer associative when using floating-point arithmetic. Also depending on the input values themselves, the best way to perform the order of operations could vary. This means that depending on how the evaluation order is set and the values are summed, the result could bear significant differences in terms of accuracy. As there are an intractable number of ways to choose the evaluation order, the task of finding the right one is almost impossible.

One consequence is that when dealing with a distributed system, the evaluation order of computations will be dependent also on the architecture used. Indeed, clustering and dispatching computations over several nodes will prevent some evaluation order being achieved. For example, when dealing with a very large sum of terms coming from many objects, the fog could have one node to aggregate it all. Or it could have several local nodes, on top of which another will aggregate the local sums. Even by ignoring the fact that all of these aggregations would be done in an asynchronous way, the overall accuracy will be different depending on the architecture. Results will not be the same between one large sum of N terms, and k small sums of $\frac{N}{k}$ terms, aggregated at the end by another sum of k terms.

In this very small example, the difficulty is easily understandable; however, on more complex data streams, the behavior could really depend on external factors that have nothing to do with the internal computation done by each part of the system. The arrangement of the objects themselves will be significant. By looking at the fog paradigm, it is easy to assume that the configuration of the fog will be dynamic in order to allow more plasticity of the system. The number of objects, the number of layers and the role of each layer will not be known in advance, which means that there will be no way to predict how much drift computations can accumulate. It is even possible that the whole system reaches a complexity that makes it totally non-deterministic. Even when a system is stable enough to be used, any change like scaling it up could make it unstable, and there will be no easy way to know in advance. Here again, validation will be tied on human observation, with the risk that something wrong is seen only when the system has been already derailing significantly.

8.8. Quality is everything

Even when a system is designed with every good intention possible, it is difficult to build it in a fully reliable fashion. As we have seen, some mishaps can be caused by both internal issues and the external dynamic. However, the discussion about security is not to be forgotten either. Of course, there are obvious concerns about protecting unwanted takeover from outside (which is currently, at its very early stage in the industry, dwelling in the Internet of Things). Also, a new kind of threat can occur because of the ever-evolving architecture inherent in the Internet of Things. It is desirable to allow more and more data producers to join in and let their flow data in order to structure them into knowledge. However, this permissive access to the flow will probably allow new kinds of attack. This risk was not really a problem before the Internet of Things, as the cloud only had access to the storage and was able to blacklist in order to prevent unwanted users (or devices) from doing harm.

In the fog computing paradigm, any new device can access the local network exchange and start pouring in deliberately wrong data in order to make the system lose its logic. It is similar to injecting SQL code in a web request but at a more numerical approach and a more local level. When the security is centralized and the communication well bounded in advance, it is rather easy to build security protocols. Also when a system is fully specified in advance and every part of it is known and identified at the very start, any new device acting differently is automatically seen as suspicious. However, with a fully distributed and ever-adapting architecture, security is more about plasticity than the perpetuation of a known, stable and legitimate state of functioning.

One of the key aspects that will be difficult to detect will be the drift in behavior caused by either a local entity trying to fool the system or a legitimate drift in computation due to an architectural flaw. The receiving layer will really have a hard time keeping up with the situation. When things might get out of hand, it will have to shut down its own network in order to prevent contagion to further layers. Having a graduated and intelligent response will be almost intractable, and rebooting would be the only answer. This kind of drastic answer is not new, and even in the most advanced airplane systems, a regular sanitary reboot is necessary in order to purge numerical drift and the accumulation of small bugs.

With this kind of behavior, it could be difficult for any end user to feel comfortable giving complete local control to a fog when it could be shutting itself down whenever something goes wrong. This means that an end-user will want both autonomy of the system and some possible oversight when needed. This will require them to have two contradictory views of a system: a far-away view that is needed, to have only relevant knowledge aggregated and a multitude of local views in order to see where things go wrong (these ones being utterly discouraging to handle). The only way to dodge the problem is to build a coherent notion of the quality of the knowledge that is produced, which is not easy when dealing with computations. Without it, systems will be trapped between being too complex to be monitored efficiently or sometimes inherently unreliable.

When it comes to numerical safety, the problem of distant local entities handling data is that there is no clear intrinsic information about its safety. A numerical value is usually a pure raw word of 32 or 64 bits expressing a value, with nothing more about it. There is currently no protocol, no standard, to enrich this data with more metadata such as how it was produced and how much confidence one could put in it. This is surprising since for any other kind of data exchanged on the Internet (like music, video and even text), we have multiple information sources describing how the data were produced, by whom, how to use it, what right or restriction is attached to it, etc. As for numerical information, everything is still to be invented in this respect, and the need for it is far from irrelevant.

As data flow between every object in the Internet of Things, no one knows for sure on what numerical implementation it had been handled. For example, if one device decides to treat every value as a 32-bit word despite each one before and after working in 64 bits, there are 32 bits that are definitely lost but that no one suspects are lost. Fundamentally it is because no one attached information on how accurate and reliable the data are. Another example could be drawn from statistical methods. It is possible to express the confidence one can have about the average and the standard deviation of a statistical test. However, if a local entity just relays the average and the standard deviation of what it monitors, without any confidence value, then the meaning of the data is clearly diminished and the rest of the process using it could suffer. This is the kind of problem that will arise when engineers will have to handle numerical computations over a distributed architecture, without any kind of global oversight available.

By adding some information about the numerical value themselves, there is room for more local oversight and safe implementation. For example, as a numerical drift is growing, the number of significant digits will decrease over time. The metadata will reflect this evolution and the local entity aggregating these data will be aware of it and could start adapting itself and try to isolate the most faulty devices, in order to bring back balance. By pushing this line of reasoning one step further, any kind of numerical approximation should also propagate its own computing bias within its numerical outputted values. For example, a Taylor polynomial interpolation or a Newton Raphson solving iteration introduces a certain approximation from the way they are tuned.

Somehow anyone receiving an approximate value should be aware of the numerical approximation, as well as the approximation introduced by the methodology. Both can have drastic effects by amplifying one another (even though on some lucky occasions, they can cancel themselves out). This notion ultimately relates to the numerical quality of a received value. In the fog paradigm, this notion would help reduce the uncertainty of distributed calculations and improve any automatic decision process, before propagating uncertain data from one layer to another. However, this requires an important effort from normalization committees in order to introduce such a notion as a regulatory standard, which is far from being done.

8.9. Fog computing versus cloud computing and edge computing

Even if the word "computing" occurs in the names of those three architectures, these architectures are basically different, but can be associated in any information system requiring the processing of IoT data. Fog, cloud and edge computing may appear similar, but they are in fact different layers of the IoT, as illustrated in Figure 8.1.

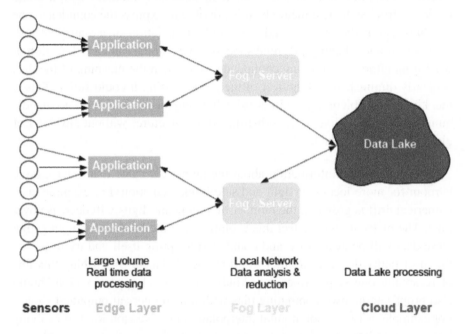

Figure 8.1. *Edge/fog/cloud computing layers. For a color version of this figure, see www.iste.co.uk/laurent/data.zip*

Most enterprises are familiar with cloud computing, which is now a *de facto* standard in many industries. Fog and edge computing are two extensions of cloud networks, which involve a collection of distributed servers. Such a network can allow an organization to greatly exceed the resources that would otherwise be available to it, freeing organizations from the requirement to keep infrastructure on site. The primary advantage of cloud-based systems is they allow data to be collected from multiple sites and devices, which is accessible anywhere in the world.

Embedded hardware obtains data from IoT devices and passes it to the fog layer. Pertinent data is then passed to the cloud layer, which is typically in a different geographical location. The cloud layer is thus able to benefit from IoT devices by receiving their data through the other layers. Organizations often achieve superior results by integrating a cloud platform with on-site fog networks or edge devices. The main difference between fog computing and cloud computing is that cloud is a centralized system, while fog is a distributed decentralized infrastructure. Fog computing is a mediator between hardware and remote servers. It regulates which information should be sent to the server and which can be processed locally.

Fog computing and edge computing appear similar since they both involve bringing intelligence and processing closer to the creation of data. However, the key difference between the two lies in where the location of intelligence and compute power is. A fog environment places intelligence at the local area network (LAN). This architecture transmits data from endpoints to a gateway, where it is then transmitted to sources for processing and return transmission. Edge computing places intelligence and processing power in devices such as embedded automation controllers.

The growth of the IoT has increased the need for edge, fog and cloud architecture, and those architectures must be studied when the data lake needs to acquire this data type.

8.10. Concluding remarks: fog computing and data lake

Fog computing proposes an alternative for data ingestion, especially for the IoT data, inside the data lake. The proposal is to aggregate and pre-calculate some indicators (already defined) based on data from sensors and only propagate those data. If we refer to the data lake definition (in Chapter 1), the foundation of the data lake is to accept raw data, the finest possible granularity, in order not to influence the future analysis and exploration of those data. The fog computing concept could not be in adequation of the data lake concept but based on practical experience and, because the fog computing produces metadata, transparency of statistical method used and the lineage of the aggregated data, this option is one to study when IoT represents an important data volume.

Fog computing represents a very interesting architecture option if there is a balance between volume and useful data to ingest into the data lake, in the case of IoT data. The cloud and edge architectures, strongly linked to fog computing, are also an interesting option for the hybrid cloud data lake, with the aim of providing storage and computation at the edge of the network that reduces network traffic and overcomes many cloud computing drawbacks. Fog computing technology helps to overcome the challenges of data lake processing.

9

The Gravity Principle in Data Lakes

We have seen in the previous chapter how the data lake concept can be complex from an architecture point of view and is not only a simple storage management system. The Apache Hadoop technology, which is the most used technology to store data for the data lake, is now not the only solution proposed. Several hybrid solutions such as NoSQL and RDBMS are now implemented. The data lake solutions are now more complex to design, from an architecture point of view, and really need to explore several technologies and approaches. In this chapter, we want to explore some factors which can force, from an architecture angle, alternative solutions to the "physical" data movement from data sources to data lakes. Based on some works in [ALR 15, MCC 14, MCC 10], an interesting perspective to explore for the data lake is the data gravity concept. In this chapter, we want to investigate what the data gravity influence could be on the data lake design architecture and which are the parameters into the data gravity concept could influence.

9.1. Applying the notion of gravitation to information systems

9.1.1. *Universal gravitation*

In physics, universal gravitation refers to the mutual attraction between any two bodies whose mass is not null. According to Newton, the force F between

Chapter written by Anne LAURENT, Thérèse LIBOUREL, Cédrine MADERA and André MIRALLES.

two point bodies of respective masses m_1 and m_2 and located at distance d is as follows:

$$F = G \cdot \frac{m_1 \cdot m_2}{d^2}$$

where G is the universal gravitational constant. Gravitation is the cause of orbital motions of the planets around the Sun, as shown in Figure 9.1.

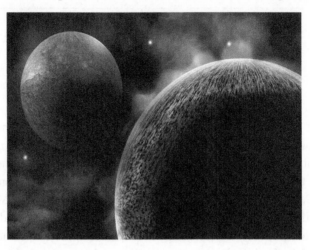

Figure 9.1. *The gravitational force keeps the planets in their orbits*

On Earth, gravity, also called heaviness, results from gravitation and is responsible of the trivial fact that objects fall down. Given an object O on Earth, the gravity (or the acceleration endured because of gravity) is:

$$Gravity_O = G \cdot \frac{M_{Earth}}{R_{Earth}^2}$$

where M_{Earth} and R_{Earth} stand respectively for the mass and the radius of Earth.

Subsequently, Einstein enhanced this theory by linking the three space dimensions to the time dimension, yielding the notion of space–time continuum. As mentioned on the Astronoo website[1] (translated from French

---

1 http://www.astronoo.com/fr/articles/espace-dans-le-temps.html.

into English by the authors): *This four-dimensional space–time fabric "looks like" the surface of a trampoline, distended by the planets and the stars. This deformation or curvature of space–time in its spatial three dimensions is responsible for gravity as felt on Earth.* An object distorts the space–time according to its mass and so, attracts other objects: the Earth is in orbit because it follows the curves of the hummocky space fabric, distorted by the presence of the Sun and other planets.

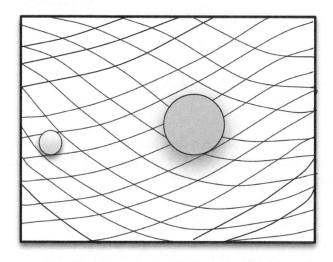

Figure 9.2. *Space–time distortion. For a color version of this figure, see www.iste.co.uk/laurent/data.zip*

In what follows, we first draw a parallel between the notion of universal gravitation in the sense of physics (as above), and the notion of gravitation in the context of Information Systems (IS).

9.1.2. *Gravitation in information systems*

Like universal gravitation in physics, gravitation in IS concerns two types of object, namely data and processes. The force can thus be exerted either between data, between processes, or between data and processes (see Figure 9.3).

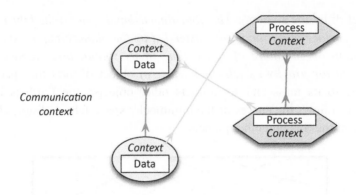

Figure 9.3. *Gravitation in an information system. For a color version of this figure, see www.iste.co.uk/laurent/data.zip*

As for the interaction between data and processes, considering Newton's formula stated previously in section 9.1, the formula defining the gravitation between data and processes in IS is given by:

$$Gravitation = G \cdot \frac{M_d \cdot M_p}{D^2}$$

where M_d and M_p denote the "mass" of data and the "mass" of processes, respectively, and where D denotes the "distance" between the data and the process.

The mass of data is computed as follows:

$$Mass_d = Volume_d \cdot Density_d$$

where $Volume_d$ stands for the *volume of data*, which accounts for the associated hard-disk space and what is called the data context (i.e., RAM and metadata), and $Density_d$ stands for the *data density*, which accounts for potential data compression (RAM and hard-disk).

The mass of processes is computed as follows:

$$Mass_p = Volume_p \cdot Density_p$$

where $Volume_p$ stands for the *volume of processes*, which accounts for the associated hard-disk memory and what is called the process context (i.e., necessary CPU), and $Density_p$ stands for the *process density*, which accounts for potential data compression (RAM and hard-disk).

The attraction exerted by processes on data can be called *process gravity* (referring to the acceleration imposed on data by the processes) and defined by:

$$G_p = G \cdot \frac{Mass_p}{D^2}$$

where D is the distance between the data and the process.

Similarly, the exerted attraction of data on the processes can be called *data gravity* (referring to the acceleration imposed on the processes because of the data) and defined by:

$$G_d = G \cdot \frac{Mass_d}{D^2}$$

where D is the distance between the data and the process.

However, the attraction exerted by one piece of data d on another piece of data d', called *data/data gravity* (referring to the acceleration imposed on one piece of data because of another piece of data) is defined by:

$$G_{dd'} = G \cdot \frac{Mass_{d'}}{D^2}$$

where D is the distance between the pieces of data d and d'.

Similarly, the attraction exerted by one process p on another process p', called *process/process gravity* (referring to the acceleration imposed on one process because of another process) is defined by:

$$G_{pp'} = G \cdot \frac{Mass_{p'}}{D^2}$$

where D is the distance between the processes p and p'.

Based on the analogy with physics, we thus have the following three cases of gravity to consider in IS:

– data/process gravity;

– data/data gravity;

– process/process gravity.

We now explain why these different cases of gravity have to be taken into account in the current systems.

By usage, operational systems are the principal data source for Decision support Information Systems (DIS). These operational systems are separated within the IS from the other components (such as DIS), not only at the application level, but also at a technical level. In the design phase of a DIS, the previous technology for operational systems did not allow us to achieve all features expected by the operational system and by the DIS, within a common architecture at the software and technical levels. Consequently, component separation within a given IS has been necessary in order to fulfill the following requirements of operational systems:

– high availability;

– real-time computing;

– backup;

– volumetry;

– reliability;

– performance;

– encryption;

– security-sensitivity;

– updateability-scalability.

Operational systems focus their computing power on transactions because they require highly available real-time resources. Their efficiency can be lowered when processing specifically organized data, redundant data, or even data requiring expensive transformations. Consequently, the split of the component architectures of the IS implies that the data of the operational system have to be duplicated in order to feed the DIS. As currently, DIS do not have to meet such high availability requirements, this technical split was imposed for DIS only. Thus, instead of keeping the data next to the operational system, it has been proposed to keep the system away from where data are produced. The notions of data ingestion, replication, propagation and integration have been introduced to characterize the data stream between the place where data are produced and the place data are used.

However, because of the development of data access, due to a significant increase in IS users, and of the huge volumes of data now available, expectations related to DIS tend to meet those related to operational systems regarding availability, expandability, performance, reliability and particularly real-time computing, which impose additional constraints to DIS. Since access to information through IS increases, processes using data also increase, and this yields important data replication which, in turn, implies potential problems regarding not only data quality and reliability, but also security.

In parallel to this change in DIS usage, technical progress now allows particular types of operational systems to merge their own data-processes with those of the DIS, thus avoiding costly data replications inside the IS. Such technical evolution gives rise to new options regarding the "cohabitation" of operational system with DIS, both sharing the same technical architecture. Such technical architectures, called HATP (*Hybrid Transactional Analytical Processing*) [GAR 16], open up the possibility of avoiding systematic data transfer for processing.

It is thus important to re-consider systematic data replication and transfer for processing, and to design new systems that would take into account data-process gravitation. Section 9.2 deals with our work on the impact of gravitation on the architecture of data lakes.

9.2. Impact of gravitation on the architecture of data lakes

It seems that, from both industrial and literature points of view, the split of the technical architecture from the data sources has been commonly acknowledged. All data to be mined or analyzed are systematically replicated, giving rise to the notion of *data container* where replicated data are physically stored. By analogy a data lake can be seen as a huge data storage space, with no replication, or as a physical data container working most of the time under the Hadoop Distributed File System (HDFS) technology. However, we emphasize that gravitation is not considered, or not even taken into account, in the definition of the applicative architectures of the data lakes and that the systematic replication of data sources should not be the standard approach. In this chapter, we would like to raise this point and show that gravitation has an important impact on the architecture of data lakes and thus, that taking this gravitation into account implies the search of a new solution, different from those based on a unique data container, as HDFS.

In [RUS 17], the author proposes alternative approaches to this HDFS based technology, among which relational and NoSQL databases are considered. In [RUS 17] and [CHE 15], the authors propose an approach in which several physical data containers under different technologies can be used within the same data lake. This approach enhances the possible architectures that could then meet the non-functional constraints of data lakes. Our point of view is similar to this work, but we go further by considering the gravitation.

Figure 9.3 shows that gravitation in the IS has to altogether take into account the contexts of the data, the process, and various parameters of the communication within the IS. The context of data includes indications from meta data describing their origin, such as sensitivity.

For example, in May 2018, the Global Data Protection Regulation (GDPR) will provide European citizens with additional rights regarding their personal data. This will significantly impact the classification of these data, which will then be classified as sensitive data. The impact will not only address security (which can be achieved using encryption), but also the fact that centralized architectures will have to be provided in order to limit data dispersion, improve data protection and optimize data management. As a consequence, the processes dealing with these data will have to move next to them.

However, the context of process depends on the underlying processor and on its sensitivity, whereas the context of data communication depends on the type of network (wired, WiFi, etc.) on which data are transferred.

Continuing the analogy with physics, air friction, that impacts the speed of bodies, can be compared with the notion of context of communication that would either accelerate or slow, if not prevent, the movement of data between data and processes.

Regarding the attraction between data and processes, if the data gravity increases because of the mass, moving or replicating these data becomes impossible, and this implies that these data attract the processes. Similarly, if process gravity increases (because of the mass) data are attracted because processes cannot be moved. We give more details on these two issues below.

9.2.1. *The case where data are not moved*

In our experiments, we observed that at least two factors impact data gravity, namely:

– the mass;

– the context, especially data sensitivity.

Recalling that data gravity G_d was defined in section 9.1 by:

$$G_d = G \cdot \frac{Mass_d}{D^2}$$

where $Mass_d$ is the mass of data, when this mass increases, data cannot be moved and processes are attracted to them. This is, for example, what happens when the size of a data source becomes too large, or when the production frequency induces huge volumes of data whose replication in the infrastructure of the data lake is impossible. Any process aiming at handling this data source will have to move where the data are stored, as depicted in Figure 9.4.

Fog computing ([ROU 17a]) accounts for this feature because processes are partly moved to the data sources, when data volumes are too high for replication. The emergence of "smart" sensors that integrate some pre-processing in order to replicate "relevant" data only implicitly illustrates the effect of data gravity over processes.

Intrinsically, data lakes access brute data, in their original format. So, when data gravity is high, processes are moved next to these data and the process output is stored in the data lake. It should thus be clear that the applicative and technical architecture of data lakes has to take this phenomenon into account. For example, in tools like Apache Spark, data are accessed in a federated mode, processed where they are and then the results are exported in the data lake.

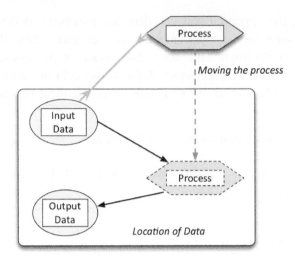

Figure 9.4. *Data-process attraction. For a color version of this figure, see www.iste.co.uk/laurent/data.zip*

Figure 9.5 shows an example of a data lake structure in which processes are moved where data are stored and in which data are replicated within the data lake. We call such a scenario *hybrid mode of data lake structure*.

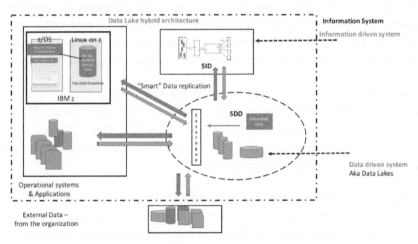

Figure 9.5. *Hybrid architecture of data lakes. For a color version of this figure, see www.iste.co.uk/laurent/data.zip*

9.2.2. *The case where processes are not moved*

Data lakes might have to use their own processes or already existing processes. Similarly to the previous case, we identified the following two factors that might impact process gravity:

– complexity;

– context, especially data sensitivity.

The complexity of a process can for instance come from the underlying algorithm, or from the number of data sources involved, or even from the resources needed for its execution (an example of such a resource is the computing power). These factors have an impact on gravity, and give processes a force by which data are attracted. If the process lies within the data lake, data are attracted and, depending on the strength of the corresponding force between data and process, the data might be replicated. Another scenario is when the process lies out of the data lake, which is the case for cloud computing or for web services. In this case, the data lake takes the necessary data next to the process and exports the process output only. Its complexity increases the process mass and so, makes it more important

Based on the following formula given in section 9.1:

$$G_p = G \cdot \frac{Mass_p}{D^2}$$

where $Mass_p$ is the process mass, we can state that if the complexity has an impact on the mass then complexity has an impact on process gravity, implying that process attracts data.

Process sensitivity is another factor that impacts process gravity. When sensitivity becomes very high, the mass increases in such a way that the process cannot be moved, and due to its gravity, it attracts data. For example, a process that outputs sensitive data has to be secured, or if the underlying algorithm contains confidential formulas, the process cannot be moved. We also note that the case of GDPR also concerns processes. Indeed, when the data used by the process are not sensitive by themselves, it can be that the output data are sensitive. The process is then seen as sensitive and in this case, due to the gravity, the input data will have to be moved next to the process.

9.2.3. *The case where the environment blocks the move*

When considering gravitation, the environment in which the bodies lie is also important. Therefore, continuing our analogy between physics and IS, the impact of the environment of data and processes must be considered. This is because this environment can accelerate, slow or even block some moves of data or processes.

When data are moved, and thus replicated, the transfer induces a production cost and a moving cost that depend on the environment. These costs reflect the impact of the environment in slowing the data moves, and thus in enforcing processes to move.

Indeed, the provision of data or data sources has a cost for the system that hosts or emits these data, at the storage level (even for temporary storage), and also at the level of hardware capability (memory, processing units, etc.). So, the data provision is less efficient when the system has to face too many requests, considering, in addition, the ever increasing volumes of data to process. It should be clear that, in this scenario the environment plays a key role and thus, has to be carefully taken into account in the study of IS gravity. In particular, the impact on the environment of systematically replicating the data provided to a data lake has to be carefully assessed when designing the applicative and technical architecture.

A similar reasoning holds for processes and their environment. For example, the cost of data processing can be lowered if the process is run in its own environment, or in an external environment of type "cloud". In this case, process gravity will tend to let the data be moved next to the process, and so, the environment accelerates this phenomenon.

At a conceptual level, we also consider the case where the environment prevents any move of either data or of processes. Highly secured environments illustrate this point, because these environments enforce a clear and strong separation between data and processes, making it impossible to either of them to be next to the other, by means of a data lake. For example, accessing data through WiFi might induce a strong resistance of the environment, thus preventing the data or the processes from moving.

To sum up, we have stated the importance of the three-fold context: data, process and environment, when taking into account the gravity in a data lake. In our point of view, the design of a data lake must involve the notion of gravitation in order to guarantee quality and security of the lifecycles of data, processes and their environments.

Glossary

This glossary gathers definitions of terms used in this book. These definitions are borrowed from the bibliographical sources and from the corporate terminology in use at IBM.

Business Intelligence

Business intelligence (BI) refers to the strategies and technologies used by organizations for data analysis of business information. Historically, it was synonymous with data warehousing; however, today, it more often refers to the analysis and reporting of data once it has been curated in a data warehouse or other data analytical platform. Similarly, BI tools refer to the software primarily used and business functions for reporting, visualization, creating dashboards and data analysis. These tools are typically used against data that has already been prepared for reporting and analysis (data marts); in contrast, data science involves a measure of data manipulation and, in some cases, acquiring data before analysis. In addition to statistical data analysis, data science may also involve aspects of machine learning.

Data Architecture

Data architecture plays an increasingly important role and has evolved to consider all areas of data management, not just relational database storage. It defines an organization's data strategy, covering decisions on the different types of data store (relation, NoSQL), data integration strategies (messaging, streaming, API, batch files) and data security. Data architecture also encompasses the design of data stores (data modeling) and defines standards for data modeling.

Data Catalog

The aim of a *data catalog* is to allow data analysts to locate the data required for their analysis. The catalog then describes the data and where it is located, and may also define how it can be accessed. A data catalog is used to bring together related data that may be hosted in different repositories to make it easier for analysts to retrieve data.

Data Engineering

Data engineering is the process of managing data as a whole. In some cases, it just refers to the process of moving data from one data store to another, usually with some data transformation or integration. In other cases, it refers to all aspects, including defining data stores (data architecture, data modeling) and data security.

Data Governance

Data governance is the overall management of data availability, relevancy, usability, integrity and security in an enterprise. Data governance practices provide a holistic approach to managing, improving and leveraging information to increase the overall data management efficiency of an enterprise.

Data Integration

A *data integration* process moves data from one system to another. For small data volumes, this can be implemented using messaging technology or APIs. For large data volumes, data integration involves batch files or data streaming technologies.

Data Lineage

Data lineage identifies the root source of data (golden record, authoritative source) and the target system, and documents the transformations applied to the data.

Data Mart

A *data mart* is a collection of information organized in a dimensional structure to support a specific use case or related use cases.

Data Model

A *data model* describes and organizes data, and defines how they relate to each other and to real world entities. A data model explicitly determines the structure of data. Data models are specified in a data modeling notation, which is often in graphical form.

Data Pipelines

A *data pipeline* is a new term, used to describe the movement of data from a source system to an analytical system. It is often used in Big Data platforms and is analogous to data integration and ETL.

Data Quality

Data quality enables us to cleanse data and monitor data quality on an ongoing basis, ensuring that the data is trusted by checking factors such as accuracy, completeness, relevance and age. Data quality is an essential characteristic that determines the reliability of data for decision-making. Typically, it involves data stewards who are empowered with improving data quality.

Data Science

Data science refers to scientific methods to extract knowledge and insight from data.

Data Steward

A *data steward* is a role within an organization responsible for using data governance processes to ensure the fitness of data elements – both the content and metadata.

Data Store

In many respects, *data store* is a synonym for database; it is gaining usage to indicate any type of system used to store data, as database tends to have connotations of relational database systems.

Derived Data

Derived data are data obtained from atomic data typically described by a business rule. For example, if a business rule stipulates that value added tax is charged at 20%, then the tax amount is derived from the sales amount.

ETL

ETL or Extract, Transform and Load refers to three stages in data warehousing: extract from source, transform data and load to target.

Information Catalog

The information catalog is an index that describes document repositories and data stores, allowing users to retrieve and locate information.

Information Life-cycle Governance

Information life-cycle governance or ILG helps organizations manage their business information throughout its lifecycle – from creation to deletion. ILG addresses the problems that challenge records management, electronic discovery, compliance, storage optimization and data migration initiatives.

Machine Learning

Machine learning is a form of AI that enables a system to learn from data rather than only through explicit programming.

Master Data

Master data refers to high-value operational information that needs to be maintained and shared in a consistent and managed way. Master data management is the process of identifying, curating, integrating and sharing master data.

Metadata

Metadata has traditionally been described as information about data. It is an information layer that describes (a) the systems that process and store data along with (b) the structure, content, meaning, relationship and lineage of the data.

NoSQL

NoSQL is a generic term for all data stores that do not use SQL – or that do not only use SQL. There are different types of NoSQL data stores, including key-value, graph, column and document. For many of today's applications – which are built from components using different programming languages and connected using web service calls and APIs – a multi-data store approach is far better than a "monolithic" data layer, which uses just one data store system to meet the demands for flexibility and scalability.

Ontology

An *ontology* provides a formal naming, and definition of data within a domain. It also defines the categories, properties and relationships between data and can extend to include concepts and entities that are also included in the domain. An organization typically has more than one ontology, for example an ontology can define the data used within an organization's finance department and that used within research and development. An ontology often extends outside an organization and facilitates communication between organizations, for example, the disease ontology. Knowledge graph is sometimes used as a synonym for ontology.

Reference Data Management

Reference data are data that define a set of permissible values to be used by other data fields. Reference data gain in value when they are widely reused and referenced. Typically, they do not change overly much in terms of definition, apart from occasional revisions. Reference data are often defined by standard organizations, such as country codes. Reference data management is therefore the process of identifying, curating, integrating and sharing reference data.

Taxonomy

A *taxonomy* provides the hierarchical classification of entities of interest to an organization. It also defines the rules by which entities are classified. Applying rigor in specification, it ensures that any newly discovered object is fit into one and only one category or object. Within a taxonomy, entities at the top of the hierarchy are abstract and general, and those at the bottom are more precise and specific.

References

[ABA 14] ABADI D., AGRAWAL R., AILAMAKI A., "The beckman report on database research", *ACM SIGMOD Record*, vol. 43, no. 3, pp. 61–70, ACM, 2014.

[ABD 16] ABDELHEDI F., AIT BRAHIM A., ATIGUI F. *et al.*, "Processus de transformation MDA d'un schéma conceptuel de données en un schéma logique NoSQL", *34e Informatique des Organisations et Systèmes d'Information et de Décision (INFORSID 2016)*, Grenoble, France, pp. 15–30. Available at: Conghttps://www.overleaf.com/project/5d2369169f5f9f14b2dc2e3a/file/5d89b8fcfa5b4000 01ac1996rès, May 2016.

[ALR 15] ALREHAMY H., WALKER C., "Personal data lake with data gravity pull", *Proceedings 2015 IEEE Fifth International Conference on Big Data and Cloud Computing Bdcloud 2015*, pp.160–167, 2015.

[ALS 16] ALSERAFI A., ABELLÓ A., ROMERO O. *et al.*, "Towards information profiling: Data lake content metadata management", *16th International Conference on Data Mining Workshops (ICDMW)*, IEEE, pp. 178–185, 2016.

[ANS 18] ANSARI J.W., Semantic profiling in data lake, PhD thesis, RWTH Aachen University, 2018.

[ARE 14] ARENAS M., DAENEN J., NEVEN F. *et al.*, "Discovering XSD keys from XML data", *ACM Transactions on Database Systems (TODS)*, vol. 39, no. 4, p. 28, ACM, 2014.

[BER 07] BERNSTEIN P.A., MELNIK S., "Model management 2.0: Manipulating richer mappings", *Proceeding of SIGMOD*, Beijing, China, pp. 1–12, 2007.

[BER 09] BERNERS-LEE T., "Linked-data design issues", W3C design issue document. Available at: http://www.w3.org/DesignIssue/LinkedData.html, June 2009.

[BEY 11] BEYER K.S., ERCEGOVAC V., GEMULLA R. *et al.*, "Jaql: A scripting language for large scale semistructured data analysis", *PVLDB*, vol. 4, no. 12, pp. 1272–1283, 2011.

[BIL 16] BILALLI B., ABELLÓ A., ALUJA-BANET T. *et al.*, "Towards intelligent data analysis: The metadata challenge", *Proceedings of the International Conference on Internet of Things and Big Data*, pp. 331–338, Rome, Italy, 2016.

[BOC 15] BOCI E., THISTLETHWAITE S., "A novel big data architecture in support of ADS-B data analytic", *Procceding Integrated Communication, Navigation, and Surveillance Conference (ICNS)*, pp. C1-1–C1-8, April 2015.

[BOU 11] BOULAKIA S.C., LESER U., "Next generation data integration for Life Sciences", *Proceeding of ICDE*, pp. 1366–1369, 2011.

[BUI 13] BUIL ARANDA C., PRUD'HOMMEAUX E., SPARQL 1.1 Federated Query, W3C recommendation, W3C. Available at: http://www.w3.org/TR/2013/REC-sparql11-federated-query-20130321/, March 2013.

[CAL 12] CALVANESE D., DE GIACOMO G., LENZERINI M. *et al.*, "Query processing under glav mappings for relational and graph databases", *Proceedings of the VLDB Endowment*, vol. 6, no. 2, pp. 61–72, VLDB Endowment, 2012.

[CAM 15] CAMPBELL C., "Top five differences between data lakes and data warehouse". Available at: https://www.blue-granite.com/blog/bid/402596/Top-Five-Differences-between-Data-Lakes-and-Data-Warehouses, January 2015.

[CAR 18] CARBONNEL J., L'analyse formelle de concepts : un cadre structurel pour l'étude de la variabilité de familles de logiciels, PhD thesis, LIRMM, Montpellier, 2018.

[CAS 16] CASTELLTORT A., MADERA C., "De l'apport des lacs de données pour les observatoires scientifiques", *Atelier SAGEO*, p. 7, December 2016.

[CHA 17] CHAHBANDARIAN G., BRICON-SOUF N., MEGDICHE I. *et al.*, "Predicting the encoding of secondary diagnoses. An experience based on decision trees", *Ingénierie des Systèmes d'Information*, vol. 22, no. 2, p. 69, Lavoisier, 2017.

[CHE 14] CHESSELL M., SCHEEPERS F., NGUYEN N. *et al.*, "Governing and managing big data for analytics and decision makers". Available at: http://www.redbooks.ibm.com/redpapers/pdfs/redp5120.pdf, August 2014.

[CHE 15] CHESSELL M., JONES N.L., LIMBURN J. *et al.*, "Designing and operating a data reservoir", *IBM Redbooks*, May 2015.

[CHU 13] CHU X., ILYAS I.F., PAPOTTI P., "Holistic data cleaning: Putting violations into context", *Procceding of the 29th International Conference on Data Engineering (ICDE)*, pp. 458–469, 2013.

[CLE 01] CLEMENTS P., NORTHROP L., *Software Product Lines: Practices and Patterns*, Addison-Wesley Professional, 3rd edition, Boston, MA, USA, 2001.

[CUR 13] CURINO C., MOON H.J., DEUTSCH A. *et al.*, "Automating the database schema evolution process", *VLDB J.*, vol. 22, no. 1, pp. 73–98, 2013.

[DAG 18] DAGA E., GANGEMI A., MOTTA E., "Reasoning with data flows and policy propagation rules", *Semantic Web*, vol. 9, no. 2, pp. 163–183, 2018.

[DAL 13] DALLACHIESA M., EBAID A., ELDAWY A. *et al.*, "NADEEF: A commodity data cleaning system", *Proceedings of the 2013 ACM SIGMOD International Conference on Management of Data, SIGMOD'13*, ACM, New York, USA, pp. 541–552, 2013.

[DAQ 17] D'AQUIN M., ADAMOU A., DIETZE S. *et al.*, "AFEL: Towards measuring online activities contributions to self-directed learning", in KRAVCIK M., MIKROYANNIDIS A., PAMMER-SCHINDLER V. *et al.* (eds), *Proceedings of the 7th Workshop on Awareness and Reflection in Technology Enhanced Learning Co-located with the 12th European Conference on Technology Enhanced Learning (EC-TEL 2017), Tallinn, Estonia, September 12, 2017.*, vol. 1997 of *CEUR Workshop Proceedings*. Available at: CEUR-WS.org, 2017.

[DEL 12] DELFOSSE V., BILLEN R., LECLERCQ P., "UML as a schema candidate for graph databases", *NoSql Matters 2012*. Available at: http://hdl.handle.net/2268/124328, 2012.

[DIX 10] DIXON J., "Pentaho, Hadoop, and Data Lakes". Available at: https://jamesdixon.wordpress.com/2010/10/14/pentaho-hadoop-and-data-lakes/, 2010.

[DON 15] DONG X.L., SRIVASTAVA D., *Big Data Integration*, Morgan & Claypool Publishers, 2015.

[DOU 15] DOUGLAS C., CURINO C., "Blind men and an elephant coalescing open-source, academic, and industrial perspectives on BigData", *Procceding ICDE*, pp. 1523–1526, 2015.

[DUL 15] DULL T., "Data lake vs data warehouse: Key differences", *KDnuggets*. Available at: https://www.kdnuggets.com/2015/09/data-lake-vs-data-warehouse-key-differences.html, September 2015.

[DUV 02] DUVAL E., HODGINS W., SUTTON S. *et al.*, "Metadata principles and practicalities", *D-lib Magazine*, vol. 8, no. 4, pp. 1082–9873, Citeseer, 2002.

[ERL 16] ERL T., KHATTAK W., BUHLER P., *Big Data Fundamentals: Concepts, Drivers & Techniques*, Prentice Hall Press, Upper Saddle River, NJ, USA, 2016.

[FAN 15] FANG H., "Managing data lakes in big data era: What's a data lake and why has it became popular in data management ecosystem?", *International Conference on Cyber Technology in Automation, Control, and Intelligent Systems (CYBER)*, IEEE, pp. 820–824, 2015.

[FED 17] FEDERICO C., SCOTT G., *Understanding Metadata*, O'Reilly Media, 2017.

[FER 15] FERNANDEZ R.C., PIETZUCH P.R., KREPS J. *et al.*, "Liquid: Unifying nearline and offline big data integration", *CIDR 2015, 7th Biennial Conference on Innovative Data Systems Research*, 2015.

[FIS 10] FISCHER P.M., ESMAILI K.S., MILLER R.J., "Stream schema: Providing and exploiting static metadata for data stream processing", *Proceedings of the 13th International Conference on Extending Database Technology, EDBT'10*, pp. 207–218, ACM, New York, USA, 2010.

[FLO 13] FLORESCU D., FOURNY G., "JSONiq: The history of a query language", *IEEE Internet Computing*, vol. 17, no. 5, pp. 86–90, 2013.

[FOS 07] FOSHAY N., MUKHERJEE A., TAYLOR A., "Does data warehouse end-user metadata add value?", *Communications of the ACM*, vol. 50, no. 11, pp. 70–77, ACM, 2007.

[FRA 05] FRANKLIN M., HALEVY A., MAIER D., "From databases to dataspaces: A new abstraction for information management", *SIGMOD Record*, vol. 34, no. 4, pp. 27–33, ACM, 2005.

[GAB 10] GABRIEL R., HOPPE T., PASTWA A., "Classification of metadata categories in data warehousing: A generic approach", *AMCIS*, p. 133, 2010.

[GAN 99] GANTER B., WILLE R., *Formal Concept Analysis: Mathematical Foundations*, Springer, 1999.

[GAR 11] GARTNER, "BIG DATA 3Vs". Available at: https://www.gartner.com/newsroom/id/1731916, 2011.

[GAR 14] GARTNER, "Gartner says beware of the data lake fallacy". Available at: http://www.gartner.com/newsroom/id/2809117, 2014.

[GAR 16] GARTNER, "Real-time insights and decision making using hybrid streaming, in-memory computing analytics and transaction processing". Available at: https://www.gartner.com/imagesrv/media-products/pdf/Kx/KX-1-3CZ44RH.pdf, 2016.

[GEI 11] GEISLER S., WEBER S., QUIX C., "An ontology-based data quality framework for data stream applications", *Proceeding ICIQ*, 2011.

[GOT 14] GOTTLOB G., ORSI G., PIERIS A., "Query rewriting and optimization for ontological databases", *ACM Transactions on Database Systems*, vol. 39, no. 3, pp. 25:1–25:46, 2014.

[HAA 14] HAAS L.M., CEFKIN M., KIELISZEWSKI C.A. *et al.*, "The IBM research accelerated discovery lab", *SIGMOD Record*, vol. 43, no. 2, pp. 41–48, 2014.

[HAI 16] HAI R., GEISLER S., QUIX C., "Constance: An intelligent data lake system", in ÖZCAN F., KOUTRIKA G., MADDEN S. (eds), *Proceedings of the 2016 International Conference on Management of Data, SIGMOD Conference*, ACM, San Francisco, CA, USA, June 26–July 01, pp. 2097–2100, 2016.

[HAL 16a] HALEVY A.Y., KORN F., NOY N.F. *et al.*, "Goods: Organizing google's datasets", in ÖZCAN F., KOUTRIKA G., MADDEN S. (eds), *Proceedings of the 2016 International Conference on Management of Data, SIGMOD Conference*, ACM, San Francisco, CA, USA, June 26–July 01, pp. 795–806, 2016.

[HAL 16b] HALEVY A.Y., KORN F., NOY N.F. *et al.*, "Managing Google's data lake: An overview of the goods system", *IEEE Data Engineering Bulletin*, vol. 39, no. 3, pp. 5–14, 2016.

[HAR 11] HARTUNG M., TERWILLIGER J.F., RAHM E., "Recent advances in schema and ontology evolution", BELLAHSENE Z., BONIFATI A., RAHM E. (eds) *Schema Matching and Mapping*, Data-Centric Systems and Applications, pp. 149–190, Springer, 2011.

[HAR 12] HARTH A., HOSE K., SCHENKEL R., "Database techniques for linked data management", CANDAN K.S., CHEN Y., SNODGRASS R.T. (eds) *et al.*, *Proceedings of the ACM SIGMOD International Conference on Management of Data, SIGMOD 2012*, pp. 597–600, ACM, Scottsdale, AZ, USA, May 20-24, 2012.

[IBM 14] IBM, "Governing and managing big data for analytics and decision makers". Available at: http://www.redbooks.ibm.com/abstracts/redp5120.html?Open, 2014.

[INM 16] INMON B., *Data Lake Architecture: Designing the Data Lake and Avoiding the Garbage Dump*, Technics Publications LLC, 2016.

[IZQ 13] IZQUIERDO J.L.C., CABOT J., "Discovering implicit schemas in json data", *Web Engineering*, pp. 68–83, Springer, 2013.

[JAR 99] JARKE M., JEUSFELD M.A., QUIX C. *et al.*, "Architecture and quality in data warehouses: An extended repository approach", *Information Systems*, vol. 24, no. 3, pp. 229–253, 1999.

[JEF 08] JEFFERY S., Pay-as-you-go data cleaning and integration, PhD thesis, EECS Department, University of California, Berkeley, December 2008.

[KAR 13] KARÆZ Y., IVANOVA M., ZHANG Y. *et al.*, "Lazy ETL in action: ETL technology dates scientific data", *PVLDB*, vol. 6, no. 12, pp. 1286–1289, 2013.

[KAT 98] KATIC N., QUIRCHMAY G., SCHIEFER J. *et al.*, "A prototype model for data warehouse security based on metadata", *Proceedings 9th International Workshop on Database and Expert Systems Applications (Cat. No. 98EX130)*, IEEE, pp. 300–308, 1998.

[KEN 09] KENSCHE D., QUIX C., LI X. *et al.*, "Generic schema mappings for composition and query answering", *Data & Knowledge Engineering*, vol. 68, no. 7, pp. 599–621, Elsevier Science Publishers B.V., 2009.

[KWO 14] KWON O., LEE N., SHIN B., "Data quality management, data usage experience and acquisition intention of big data analytics", *International Journal of Information Management*, vol. 34, no. 3, pp. 387–394, Elsevier, 2014.

[LAP 14] LAPLANTE A., SHARMA B., *Architecting Data Lakes*, O'Reilly Media, 2014.

[LEM 84] LE MOIGNE J., *Théorie du système général: théorie de la modélisation*, Presses universitaires de France, 1984.

[LEN 02] LENZERINI M., "Data integration: A theoretical perspective", *Proceedings of the 21st ACM SIGACT-SIGMOD-SIGART Symposium on Principles of Database Systems (PODS 2002)*, pp. 233–246, ACM, 2002.

[LIU 15] LIU Z.H., GAWLICK D., "Management of flexible schema data in RDBMSs: Opportunities and limitations for NoSQL", *Proceedings of the 7th Biennial Conference on Innovative Data Systems Research (CIDR 2015)*. Available at: www.cidrdb.org, 2015.

[LLA 18] LLAVE M.R., "Data lakes in business intelligence: Reporting from the trenches", *Procedia Computer Science*, vol. 138, pp. 516–524, Elsevier, 2018.

[LOP 14] LOPEZ PINO J.L., "Metadata in business intelligence". Available at: https://www.slideshare.net/jlpino/metadata-in-business-intelligence, [accessed: February 2nd, 2018], January 2014.

[MAC 17] MACCIONI A., TORLONE R., "Crossing the finish line faster when paddling the data lake with kayak", *Proceedings of the VLDB Endowment*, vol. 10, no. 12, pp. 1853–1856, VLDB Endowment, 2017.

[MAD 16] MADERA C., LAURENT A., "The next information architecture evolution: The data lake wave", *Proceedings of the 8th International Conference on Management of Digital EcoSystems*, pp. 174–180, MEDES, New York, USA, ACM, 2016.

[MAD 17] MADERA C., LAURENT A., LIBOUREL T. *et al.*, "How can the data lake concept influence information system design for agriculture?", *EFITA CONGRESS*, Montpellier, France, July 2017.

[MAH 10] MAHMOUD H.A., ABOULNAGA A., "Schema clustering and retrieval for multi-domain pay-as-you-go data integration systems", *Proceedings SIGMOD'10*, pp. 411–422, ACM, 2010.

[MAI 17] MAIER A., "How information governance is getting analytics on big data's best friend", *EDBT 2017*, IBM Analytics, 2017.

[MAR 16a] MARKETSANDMARKETS, "Data lakes market by software". Available at: https://www. marketsandmarkets.com/Market-Reports/data-lakes-market, September 2016.

[MAR 16b] MARKETSANDMARKETS, "Data lakes market". Available at: http://www. marketsandmarkets.com/PressReleases/data-lakes.asp, 2016.

[MCC 10] MCCRORY D., "Data gravity blog mccrory". Available at: https://blog. mccrory.me/2010/12/07/data-gravity-in-the-clouds/, 2010.

[MCC 14] MCCRORY D., "Data gravity". Available at: https://datagravity.org/about/, 2014.

[MEN 17] MENON P., "Demystifying data lake architecture", in *Data Science Central*. Available at: https://www.datasciencecentral.com/profiles/blogs/demystifying-data-lake-architecture, July 2017.

[MFI 17] M-FILES.COM, "L'histoire des métadonnées". Available at: https://www.m-files.com/Content/documents/en/res/Infographic-Metadata.pdf, [accessed: 02/04/2018], 2017.

[MIL 13] MILLER J.J., "Graph database applications and concepts with Neo4j", *Proceedings of the Southern Association for Information Systems Conference*, vol. 2324, Atlanta, GA, USA, 2013.

[MIL 16] MILOSLAVSKAYA N., TOLSTOY A., "Big data, fast data and data lake concepts", *Procedia Computer Science*, vol. 88, no. 1, pp. 300–305, 2016.

[MIT 13] MITRA P., SUNDARAM G., PS S., "Just in time indexing", *arXiv preprint arXiv:1308.3679*, 2013.

[MOH 14] MOHAMED M.A., ALTRAFI O.G., ISMAIL M.O., "Relational vs. nosql databases: A survey", *International Journal of Computer and Information Technology*, vol. 3, no. 03, pp. 598–601, 2014.

[NAD 17] NADIPALLI R., *Effective Business Intelligence with QuickSight*, Packt Publishing Ltd, 2017.

[NIK 14] NIKOLIC M., ELSEIDY M., KOCH C., "LINVIEW: Incremental view maintenance for complex analytical queries", *Proceedings SIGMOD*, pp. 253–264, 2014.

[NOG 18a] NOGUEIRA I., ROMDHANE M., DARMONT J., "Modélisation des métadonnées d'un data lake en data vault", *18e conférence sur l'extraction et la gestion de connaissances (EGC 2018)*, vol. E-34 of *Revue des Nouvelles Technologies de l'Information*, pp. 257–262, Paris, France, January 2018.

[NOG 18b] NOGUEIRA I.D., ROMDHANE M., DARMONT J., "Modeling data lake metadata with a data vault", *Proceedings of the 22nd International Database Engineering & Applications Symposium*, pp. 253–261, ACM, 2018.

[ORA 15] ORAM A., *Managing the Data Lake*, O'Reilly Media, Inc., September 2015.

[ÖZC 16] ÖZCAN F., KOUTRIKA G., MADDEN S. (eds), *Proceedings of the 2016 International Conference on Management of Data, SIGMOD Conference 2016*, ACM, San Francisco, CA, USA, June 26 –July 01, 2016.

[PAS 15] PASUPULETI P., PURRA B.S., *Data Lake Development with Big Data : Explore Architectural Approaches to Building Data Lakes That Ingest, Index, Manage, and Analyze Massive Amounts of Data Using Big Data Technologies*, Packt Publishing, Birmingham, UK, 2015.

[PHA 16] PHAM M., BONCZ P.A., "Exploiting emergent schemas to make RDF systems more efficient", GROTH P.T., SIMPERL E., GRAY A. J.G. *et al.* (eds), *The Semantic Web – ISWC 2016 – 15th International Semantic Web Conference, Kobe, Japan, October 17–21, 2016, Proceedings, Part I*, vol. 9981 of *Lecture Notes in Computer Science*, pp. 463–479, 2016.

[PON 04] PONNIAH P., *Data Warehousing Fundamentals: A Comprehensive Guide for IT Professionals*, John Wiley & Sons, 2004.

[POW 08] POWER D.J., "Understanding data-driven decision support systems", *Information Systems Management*, vol. 25, no. 2, pp. 149–154, Taylor and Francis, 2008.

[POW 14] POWER D.J., "Using 'Big Data' for analytics and decision support", *Journal of Decision Systems*, vol. 23, no. 2, pp. 222–228, Taylor and Francis, 2014.

[PRE 11] PRESUTTI V., AROYO L., ADAMOU A. *et al.*, "Extracting core knowledge from linked data", HARTIG O., HARTH A., SEQUEDA J.F. (eds), *Proceedings of the 2nd International Workshop on Consuming Linked Data (COLD2011)*, vol. 782 of *CEUR Workshop Proceedings*. Available at: CEUR-WS.org, Bonn, Germany, October 23, 2011.

[QUI 16] QUIX C., HAI R., VATOV I., "GEMMS: A generic and extensible metadata management system for data lakes", ESPAÑA S., IVANOVIC M., SAVIC M. (eds), *Proceedings of the CAiSE'16 Forum, at the 28th International Conference on Advanced Information Systems Engineering (CAiSE 2016)*, vol. 1612 of *CEUR Workshop Proceedings*. Available at: CEUR-WS.org, pp. 129–136, Ljubljana, Slovenia, June 13–17, 2016.

[RAV 19a] RAVAT F., ZHAO Y., "Data lakes: Trends and perspectives", *International Conference on Database and Expert Systems Applications*, pp. 304–313, Springer, 2019.

[RAV 19b] RAVAT F., ZHAO Y., "Metadata management for data lakes", *East European Conference on Advances in Databases and Information Systems*, Springer, 2019.

[RIC 14] RICHTER S., QUIANÉ-RUIZ J., SCHUH S. *et al.*, "Towards zero-overhead static and adaptive indexing in Hadoop", *VLDB J.*, vol. 23, no. 3, pp. 469–494, 2014.

[RIL 04] RILEY J., *Understanding Metadata*, NISO Press, Bethesda, MD, USA, 2004.

[RIL 17] RILEY J., *Understanding metadata: What is metadata, and what is it for?*, National Information Standards Organization (NISO). Available at: https:// groups.niso.org/apps/group_public/download.php/17446/Understanding%20Metadata.pdf, January 2017.

[ROU 17a] ROUSE M., "Fog Computing", 2017.

[RUS 17] RUSSOM P., Best practices report: Data lakes: Purposes, practices, patterns, and platforms, Report, TDWI, March 29 2017.

[SAH 14] SAHA B., SRIVASTAVA D., "Data quality: The other face of big data", *Proceeding ICDE*, pp. 1294–1297, 2014.

[SAH 18] SAHATQIJA K., AJDARI J., ZENUNI X. *et al.*, "Comparison between relational and NOSQL databases", *41st International Convention on Information and Communication Technology, Electronics and Microelectronics (MIPRO)*, IEEE, pp. 0216–0221, 2018.

[SAK 19] SAKR S., ZOMAYA A.Y. (eds), *Encyclopedia of Big Data Technologies*, Springer, 2019.

[SAR 08] SARMA A.D., DONG X., HALEVY A.Y., "Bootstrapping pay-as-you-go data integration systems", *Proceeding SIGMOD*, pp. 861–874, 2008.

[SAW 19] SAWADOGO P., KIBATA T., DARMONT J., "Metadata management for textual documents in data lakes", *21st International Conference on Enterprise Information Systems (ICEIS 2019)*, 2019.

[SEL 96] SELIGMAN L., ROSENTHAL A., "A metadata resource to promote data integration", *Proceeding of IEEE Metadata Conference*, Silver Spring, MD, 1996.

[SER 10] SERVIGNE S., "Conception, architecture et urbanisation des systèmes d'information", *Encyclopædia Universalis*, pp. 1–15, 2010.

[SHE 90] SHETH A.P., LARSON J.A., "Federated database systems for managing distributed, heterogeneous, and autonomous databases", *ACM Computing Surveys*, vol. 22, no. 3, pp. 183–236, 1990.

[SHI 06] SHIMAZU K., ARISAWA T., SAITO I., "Interdisciplinary contents management using 5W1H interface for metadata", *2006 IEEE/WIC/ACM International Conference on Web Intelligence (WI 2006 Main Conference Proceedings) (WI'06)*, IEEE, pp. 909–912, 2006.

[STA 19a] STAFF A., "ArangoDB Enterprise: Security". Available at: https://www.arangodb. com/why-arangodb/arangodb-enterprise/arangodb-enterprise-security/, [accessed: March 20th, 2019], 2019.

[STA 19b] STAFF N., "Security". Available at: https://neo4j.com/docs/operations-manual/ current/security/, [accessed March 20th, 2019], 2019.

[STE 14] STEIN B., MORRISON A., "The enterprise data lake: Better integration and deeper analytics". Available at: http://www.pwc.com/us/en/technology-forecast/2014/cloud-computing/assets/pdf/pwc-technology-forecast-data-lakes.pdf, 2014.

[STO 13] STONEBRAKER M., BESKALES G., PAGAN A. *et al.*, "Data curation at scale: The data tamer system", *CIDR 2013*, 2013.

[STO 14] STONEBRAKER M., "Why the 'Data Lake' is really a 'Data Swamp'", Blog@CACM. Available at: http://cacm.acm.org/blogs/blog-cacm/181547-why-the-data-lake-is-really-a-data-swamp/fulltext, December 2014.

[SUR 16] SURIARACHCHI I., PLALE B., "Provenance as essential infrastructure for data lakes", MATTOSO M., GLAVIC B. (eds), *Provenance and Annotation of Data and Processes*, Cham, Springer International Publishing, pp. 178–182, 2016.

[TEA 17] TEAM M.A., "Data catalog". Available at: https://azure.microsoft.com/fr-fr/services/data-catalog/, August 2017.

[TEA 18a] TEAM LAB P., "PerSCiDO". Available at: https://persyval-platform.univ-grenoble-alpes.fr/0/searchbyrecentl, [accessed: February 2nd, 2018], 2018.

[TEA 18b] TEAM A.A., "Apache atlas - data governance and metadata framework for hadoop". Available at: http://atlas.apache.org/, [accessed: February 2nd, 2018], January 2018.

[TEA 18c] TEAM T., "What is a Data Catalog?". Available at: https://www.techopedia.com/definition/32034/data-catalog, [accessed: February 2nd, 2018], 2018.

[TER 15] TERRIZZANO I.G., SCHWARZ P.M., ROTH M. *et al.*, "Data wrangling: The challenging journey from the wild to the lake", *CIDR 2015, 7th Biennial Conference on Innovative Data Systems Research*, 2015.

[THE 17] THE DATA GOVERNANCE INSTITUTE, "The DGI data governance framework". Available at: http://www.datagovernance.com/the-dgi-framework/, [accessed: February 5th, 2018], 2017.

[VAN 17] VANDENBUSSCHE P., ATEMEZING G., POVEDA-VILLALÓN M. *et al.*, "Linked open vocabularies (LOV): A gateway to reusable semantic vocabularies on the Web", *Semantic Web*, vol. 8, no. 3, pp. 437–452, 2017.

[VAR 14] VARGA J., ROMERO O., PEDERSEN T.B. *et al.*, "Towards next generation BI systems: The analytical metadata challenge", *International Conference on Data Warehousing and Knowledge Discovery*, pp. 89–101, Springer, 2014.

[VIC 10] VICKNAIR C., MACIAS M., ZHAO Z. *et al.*, "A comparison of a graph database and a relational database: A data provenance perspective", *Proceedings of the 48th Annual Southeast Regional Conference*, p. 42, ACM, 2010.

[WAL 15] WALKER C., ALREHAMY H., "Personal data lake with data gravity pull", *5th International Conference on Big Data and Cloud Computing*, pp. 160–167, IEEE, 2015.

[WAN 15] WANG L., ZHANG S., "Schema management for document stores", *Proceedings of the VLDB Endowment*, vol. 8, no. 9, pp. 922–933, VLDB Endowment, 2015.

[WHI 09] WHITE T., *Hadoop: The Definitive Guide*, O'Reilly Media, Inc., 2009.

[WIK 16] WIKIPEDIA, "Base de connaissance". Available at: fr.wikipedia.org/wiki/Base_de_connaissance, June 2016.

[WIK 18] WIKIPEDIA, "Metadata". Available at: https://en.wikipedia.org/wiki/Metadata, [accessed: February 4th, 2018], January 2018.

[WOO 11] WOODS D., "Big data requires a big, new architecture", Forbes CIO Network, 2011.

List of Authors

Alessandro ADAMOU
Data Science Institute
Insight Centre for Data Analytics
National University of Ireland
Galway
Ireland

Houssem CHIHOUB
LIG
CNRS, Grenoble INP, Inria,
Université Grenoble Alpes
France

Christine COLLET†
LIG
CNRS, Grenoble INP, Inria,
Université Grenoble Alpes
France

Mathieu D'AQUIN
Data Science Institute
Insight Centre for Data Analytics
National University of Ireland
Galway
Ireland

Rihan HAI
Informatik 5
RWTH Aachen University
Germany

Marianne HUCHARD
LIRMM
University of Montpellier, CNRS
France

Arnault IOUALALEN
Numalis
Montpellier
France

Anne LAURENT
LIRMM
University of Montpellier, CNRS
France

Dominique LAURENT
ETIS
Cergy-Pontoise University, CNRS
France

Thérèse LIBOUREL
Espace-Dev
University of Montpellier
France

Cédrine MADERA
IBM Global Market
Montpellier
France

Imen MEGDICHE
IRIT
University Paul Sabatier, CNRS
Toulouse
France

André MIRALLES
TETIS
University of Montpellier,
AgroParisTech, SIRAD, CNRS,
INRAE
France

Christoph QUIX
Hochschule Niederrhein
University of Applied Sciences
Krefeld
Germany

Franck RAVAT
IRIT
University Paul Sabatier, CNRS
Toulouse
France

Asma ZGOLLI
LIG
CNRS, Grenoble INP, Inria,
Université Grenoble Alpes
France

Yan ZHAO
IRIT
University Paul Sabatier, CNRS
Toulouse
France

Index

Other titles from

in

Computer Engineering

2020

OULHADJ Hamouche, DAACHI Boubaker, MENASRI Riad
Metaheuristics for Robotics
(Optimization Heuristics Set – Volume 2)

SADIQUI Ali
Computer Network Security

2019

BESBES Walid, DHOUIB Diala, WASSAN Niaz, MARREKCHI Emna
Solving Transport Problems: Towards Green Logistics

CLERC Maurice
Iterative Optimizers: Difficulty Measures and Benchmarks

GHLALA Riadh
Analytic SQL in SQL Server 2014/2016

TOUNSI Wiem
Cyber-Vigilance and Digital Trust: Cyber Security in the Era of Cloud Computing and IoT

2018

ANDRO Mathieu
Digital Libraries and Crowdsourcing
(Digital Tools and Uses Set – Volume 5)

ARNALDI Bruno, GUITTON Pascal, MOREAU Guillaume
Virtual Reality and Augmented Reality: Myths and Realities

BERTHIER Thierry, TEBOUL Bruno
From Digital Traces to Algorithmic Projections

CARDON Alain
Beyond Artificial Intelligence: From Human Consciousness to Artificial Consciousness

HOMAYOUNI S. Mahdi, FONTES Dalila B.M.M.
Metaheuristics for Maritime Operations
(Optimization Heuristics Set – Volume 1)

JEANSOULIN Robert
JavaScript and Open Data

PIVERT Olivier
NoSQL Data Models: Trends and Challenges
(Databases and Big Data Set – Volume 1)

SEDKAOUI Soraya
Data Analytics and Big Data

SALEH Imad, AMMI Mehdi, SZONIECKY Samuel
Challenges of the Internet of Things: Technology, Use, Ethics
(Digital Tools and Uses Set – Volume 7)

SZONIECKY Samuel
Ecosystems Knowledge: Modeling and Analysis Method for Information and Communication
(Digital Tools and Uses Set – Volume 6)

2017

BENMAMMAR Badr
Concurrent, Real-Time and Distributed Programming in Java

HÉLIODORE Frédéric, NAKIB Amir, ISMAIL Boussaad, OUCHRAA Salma, SCHMITT Laurent
Metaheuristics for Intelligent Electrical Networks
(Metaheuristics Set – Volume 10)

MA Haiping, SIMON Dan
Evolutionary Computation with Biogeography-based Optimization
(Metaheuristics Set – Volume 8)

PÉTROWSKI Alain, BEN-HAMIDA Sana
Evolutionary Algorithms
(Metaheuristics Set – Volume 9)

PAI G A Vijayalakshmi
Metaheuristics for Portfolio Optimization
(Metaheuristics Set – Volume 11)

2016

BLUM Christian, FESTA Paola
Metaheuristics for String Problems in Bio-informatics
(Metaheuristics Set – Volume 6)

DEROUSSI Laurent
Metaheuristics for Logistics
(Metaheuristics Set – Volume 4)

DHAENENS Clarisse and JOURDAN Laetitia
Metaheuristics for Big Data
(Metaheuristics Set – Volume 5)

LABADIE Nacima, PRINS Christian, PRODHON Caroline
Metaheuristics for Vehicle Routing Problems
(Metaheuristics Set – Volume 3)

LEROY Laure
Eyestrain Reduction in Stereoscopy

LUTTON Evelyne, PERROT Nathalie, TONDA Albert
Evolutionary Algorithms for Food Science and Technology
(Metaheuristics Set – Volume 7)

MAGOULÈS Frédéric, ZHAO Hai-Xiang
Data Mining and Machine Learning in Building Energy Analysis

RIGO Michel
Advanced Graph Theory and Combinatorics

2015

BARBIER Franck, RECOUSSINE Jean-Luc
COBOL Software Modernization: From Principles to Implementation with
the BLU AGE® Method

CHEN Ken
Performance Evaluation by Simulation and Analysis with Applications to
Computer Networks

CLERC Maurice
Guided Randomness in Optimization
(Metaheuristics Set – Volume 1)

DURAND Nicolas, GIANAZZA David, GOTTELAND Jean-Baptiste,
ALLIOT Jean-Marc
Metaheuristics for Air Traffic Management
(Metaheuristics Set – Volume 2)

MAGOULÈS Frédéric, ROUX François-Xavier, HOUZEAUX Guillaume
Parallel Scientific Computing

MUNEESAWANG Paisarn, YAMMEN Suchart
Visual Inspection Technology in the Hard Disk Drive Industry

2014

BOULANGER Jean-Louis
Formal Methods Applied to Industrial Complex Systems

BOULANGER Jean-Louis
Formal Methods Applied to Complex Systems:Implementation of the B Method

GARDI Frédéric, BENOIST Thierry, DARLAY Julien, ESTELLON Bertrand, MEGEL Romain
Mathematical Programming Solver based on Local Search

KRICHEN Saoussen, CHAOUACHI Jouhaina
Graph-related Optimization and Decision Support Systems

LARRIEU Nicolas, VARET Antoine
Rapid Prototyping of Software for Avionics Systems: Model-oriented Approaches for Complex Systems Certification

OUSSALAH Mourad Chabane
Software Architecture 1
Software Architecture 2

PASCHOS Vangelis Th
Combinatorial Optimization – 3-volume series, 2nd Edition
Concepts of Combinatorial Optimization – Volume 1, 2nd Edition
Problems and New Approaches – Volume 2, 2nd Edition
Applications of Combinatorial Optimization – Volume 3, 2nd Edition

QUESNEL Flavien
Scheduling of Large-scale Virtualized Infrastructures: Toward Cooperative Management

RIGO Michel
Formal Languages, Automata and Numeration Systems 1: Introduction to Combinatorics on Words
Formal Languages, Automata and Numeration Systems 2: Applications to Recognizability and Decidability

BOULANGER Jean-Louis
Industrial Use of Formal Methods: Formal Verification

BOULANGER Jean-Louis
Formal Method: Industrial Use from Model to the Code

CALVARY Gaëlle, DELOT Thierry, SÈDES Florence, TIGLI Jean-Yves
Computer Science and Ambient Intelligence

MAHOUT Vincent
Assembly Language Programming: ARM Cortex-M3 2.0: Organization, Innovation and Territory

MARLET Renaud
Program Specialization

SOTO Maria, SEVAUX Marc, ROSSI André, LAURENT Johann
Memory Allocation Problems in Embedded Systems: Optimization Methods

2011

BICHOT Charles-Edmond, SIARRY Patrick
Graph Partitioning

BOULANGER Jean-Louis
Static Analysis of Software: The Abstract Interpretation

CAFERRA Ricardo
Logic for Computer Science and Artificial Intelligence

HOMES Bernard
Fundamentals of Software Testing

KORDON Fabrice, HADDAD Serge, PAUTET Laurent, PETRUCCI Laure
Distributed Systems: Design and Algorithms

KORDON Fabrice, HADDAD Serge, PAUTET Laurent, PETRUCCI Laure
Models and Analysis in Distributed Systems

LORCA Xavier
Tree-based Graph Partitioning Constraint

TRUCHET Charlotte, ASSAYAG Gerard
Constraint Programming in Music

VICAT-BLANC PRIMET Pascale *et al.*
Computing Networks: From Cluster to Cloud Computing

2010

AUDIBERT Pierre
Mathematics for Informatics and Computer Science

BABAU Jean-Philippe *et al.*
Model Driven Engineering for Distributed Real-Time Embedded Systems

BOULANGER Jean-Louis
Safety of Computer Architectures

MONMARCHE Nicolas *et al.*
Artificial Ants

PANETTO Hervé, BOUDJLIDA Nacer
Interoperability for Enterprise Software and Applications 2010

SIGAUD Olivier *et al.*
Markov Decision Processes in Artificial Intelligence

SOLNON Christine
Ant Colony Optimization and Constraint Programming

AUBRUN Christophe, SIMON Daniel, SONG Ye-Qiong *et al.*
Co-design Approaches for Dependable Networked Control Systems

2009

FOURNIER Jean-Claude
Graph Theory and Applications

GUEDON Jeanpierre
The Mojette Transform / Theory and Applications

JARD Claude, ROUX Olivier
Communicating Embedded Systems / Software and Design

2005

GÉRARD Sébastien *et al.*
Model Driven Engineering for Distributed Real Time Embedded Systems

PANETTO Hervé
Interoperability of Enterprise Software and Applications 2005

Printed and bound by CPI Group (UK) Ltd, Croydon, CR0 4YY